EXPLORING WASHINGTON'S BACKROADS

Highways and Hometowns of The Evergreen State

by John Deviny

ISBN 1-59152-017-7
© 2005 John Deviny

Chapter map work derived from images provided by Raven Maps,
Medford, Oregon. All rights reserved.

Published by Wilder Productions, P.O. Box 1848, Olympia,
Washington 98507. For additional information on *Exploring
Washington's Backroads* and book ordering, visit
www.WashingtonBackroads.com.

The author recommends all readers drive carefully and within
their own and their vehicles' limitations. The safety and wisdom
of following the described routes cannot be assumed or warranted.

Created, produced, and designed in the United States.
Printed in China.

09   08   07   06   3   4   5

ACKNOWLEDGMENTS

To guides great and lesser known: Steinbeck, Kuralt, Least-Heat Moon, Satterfield, Woodbury, Horn, Robbins, Bradbury, Buffett, Keen, Henley, and all the many other gypsies and jesters who have inspired my blacktop publishing and "drive-by shootings."

To Davey and Loose, whom I met in a boxcar on my thirtieth birthday. Both were bound for someplace I so badly wanted to go—without knowing or caring where it was.

To the fine folks at Farcountry Press who inspired me and kept me on the right road as this most interesting journey unfolded.

To helpers, muses, and blind believers: Cheryl P. for her photo and design assistance; Kathie, Cherie, and others for ideas and editing; and friends and strangers whose stories I have drawn upon and perhaps stretched a bit for a comfortable fit.

And of course to Cheryl, whose encouragement and love sends me out to roam and keeps me coming home.

EXPLORING
WASHINGTON'S BACKROADS
Highways and Hometowns of The Evergreen State

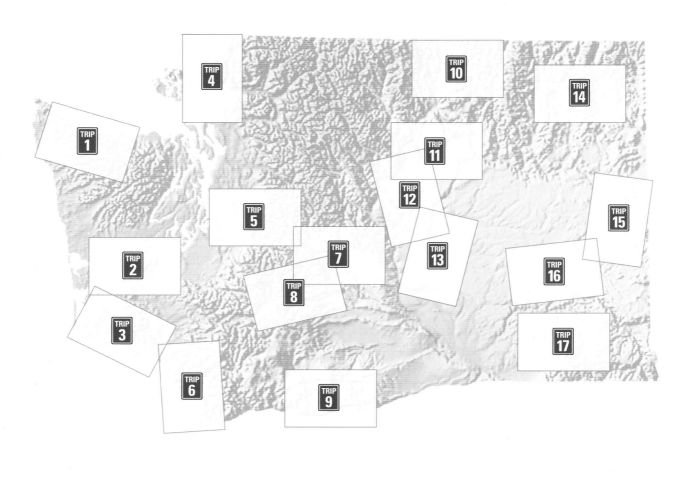

TABLE OF CONTENTS

The Olympic Range over Hood Canal tidelands

Two-lane backroads are where freedom rings and where day-to-day worries get hopelessly lost in the magic and soul of the open highway. Roadtrips have been with us since the first automobile, but the call to adventure is primitive and deep. It is our undeniable destiny to seek, to explore. And to this end we backroaders are guided by the siren song of the scenery, the curious magnetic pull of the horizon, and that glorious 26-foot-wide strip of all-knowing, never-ending asphalt.

Washington is a state of great wonder. This collection was inspired by an appreciation of our region's unique natural beauty and amazingly diverse geography. Just as much, these observations are about the people of The Evergreen State who have come here in the last century and a half—their occupations, beliefs, and cultures all adding color and definition to the landscape. I offer these pages hopeful that they will help open your eyes to the possibilities for better understanding your natural world, your neighbors, yourself.

This book is also a rebellion of sorts. A tour guide less

ordinary. It was conceived in part as a counterpoint to the growing volume of commercially fed tourist information that would take you and your wallet and deliver you to the next largely predictable, usually higher-end, often overstated, must-see destination. Here's a thought or two: The beauty around you is free! Seek the journey, not the destination. Take control, be your own tour guide, travel economy class—you'll get far closer to the action. You can embrace adventure and discovery on your own terms; all it takes is some quality time, curiosity, flexibility, and a windshield.

This guide is not intended as a script for your weekend. These roadtrip recollections are only to point you in the right direction and to inspire you. Each of the seventeen chapters is broken into sections that will back you up and urge you on as you plan your own great escapes.

Each of the seventeen journeys featured in the book has a **Sidebar,** a roadsign, if you will, that contains some brief information to get you going. You can follow me on my route or not. During much of my travel, I found myself lost—if you'll excuse the play on words. Only later would I compose a somewhat sensible course. Trust in your sense of reckoning and spirit of adventure. Backroads don't care. They simply shrug their wise shoulders and take you to where you are meant to be.

The **Essays** that wander through the heart of each chapter are my own simple observations—reflections on a sense of place at a point in time. It is always my intent to describe scenes that will beckon and please, to bring you there and draw you in. As you read you may notice that in my attempts to praise nature, solitude, and simplicity, a cynical eye is often at work. I ask that you consider, and perhaps forgive, my biases. Don't think of it as negativity,

but on-the-scene integrity! Many of us old-timers can't help but lament the obvious changes in land use, population growth, and environmental stability. And yet we also recognize that many Washingtonians are increasingly aware and protective of their surroundings, and that progress has brought a higher intelligence to the cause. It is my hope that this book and those like it will continue to stimulate respect for our natural world. You may not find this kind of thoughtfulness and honesty in your mass-market come-hither tourist trade publications! *Exploring Washington's Backroads* dares to be different. After all, where else is there a Northwest visitors guide that excludes all major cities, most of Puget Sound, any mention of the San Juans, and photographs of people!

The **Photographs** are intended to tell the story of Washington as well. The theme is quite obviously spare and simple beauty—rustic, bucolic, and all natural, except where the hand of man has gently touched the land.

With few exceptions, these images were taken without losing sight of the car. There are reasons for this. Since this is a roadtrip book, journalistic logic suggests that I display what can be seen along the highway. This is also meant to inspire you to take your own memorable shots while you follow the path, as it can easily be done: Point, hold steady, and shoot! Avoid the short-shadow part of the day. Specialized equipment? I use my sunglasses for a lens filter, fenceposts and the car roof for a tripod. I never feel a need to wake before dawn, hike for miles, and crouch in the wet grass for just the right shot. There's a road out there, darnit, and I need to be on it!

The **Maps** tend to be more art than science, and I do recommend that you throw a good road guide on the passenger seat. Unless

there's someone sitting there, in which case you have what we call a navigator. This, of course, is someone who tells you to stop and ask directions. There are plenty of alternatives to the routes described in this book. I use the *Benchmark Washington Road and Recreation Atlas* and reference its pages in each chapter sidebar. DeLorme also publishes a fine atlas, and there are a variety of state highway, forest service, and county maps that can guide you. You will also want to know more about history, geography, points of interest, and accommodations. A number of fine resources are listed at the back of this book.

A famous American novelist once wrote that small towns are "where extremes clash and mediocrity abundantly rules." In the **Hometowns** segments, I strove for a surreal snapshot of the region using a more intimate viewpoint. I have always had a blind fascination with these small communities—quaint in character and not afraid to show their age. And I presume much: that these towns are reflections of their surroundings, always friendly, of strong integrity, and united in their belief about such things as progress and righteous living. In keeping with this fantasy, the vignettes and their photos are purposely impressionistic and brief. As you drive through the hometowns on these pages, and so many more like them, remember that unlike bigger cities, their soul is on the surface. To know the depth and essence, don't look too deep. Just like when you grew up in your own hometown, truth often lives in first impressions.

Whether you are in the driver's seat or on the couch, you are now ready to take yourself away to the backroads and hometowns of Washington State.

Enjoy the ride. Drive friendly.

A fogbank hovers behind Crescent Bay on the Strait of Juan de Fuca

LOCATION:
- At the top of the Washington's Olympic Peninsula in Clallam County
- Benchmark Atlas pages 52, 53
- Route from US 101 along State Highways 112 and 113 to the Elwha River approximately 73 miles

SIGHTS AND SCENES:
- The still enigmatic Strait of Juan de Fuca, once thought to be the entrance to a sea route across the North American continent
- Lonely quiet beaches of seaweed and drift logs that hold hints of a once-bustling commerce
- The jewel of Lake Crescent at the doorstep of the rugged Olympic Mountains
- Pristine rivers flowing down ancient tree-lined valleys of unreal green

FOLLOW ME:
- From US 101 at the community of Sappho turn north on Washington Highway 113
- At the Pysht River head east on Highway 112
- Follow the Strait of Juan de Fuca east to the town of Joyce
- Find the Crescent Beach Road, which loops you to the shore at Salt Creek County Park
- Take the Hampton Road back to 112 and return west to Joyce
- Follow the Joyce-Piedmont Road to Lake Crescent, follow the north shore to the intersection with Hwy 101
- Return west on 101 to where you began or turn east to sample Olympic National Park via the Elwha River

THE STRAIT AND NARROW ROAD
To the Top of the Olympics

Kalaloch Creek fades into the Pacific shore

The year was 1932 and traffic backed up fifteen miles north to the town of Forks. Down at the Hoh River, Governor Hadley formally dedicated the bridge that would be the final connection in the Highway 101 loop around the Olympics. The loop was completed, but it wasn't easy. Nothing ever is up here.

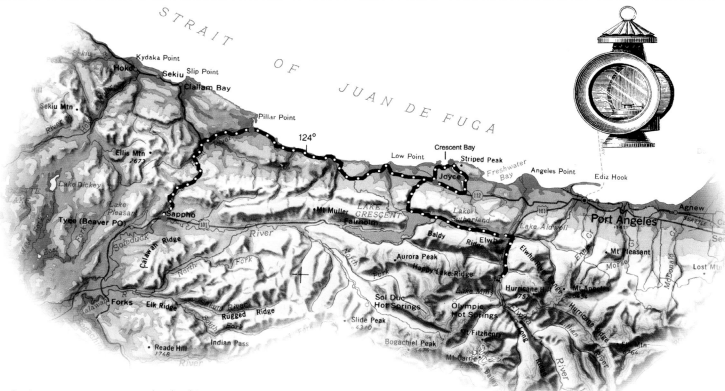

Tough pioneers met an even tougher land in the 1800s. Lusting for timber, all they could see through the constant rain was a place boggy and thick, bigger and more rugged and more impossibly impassable than imagined. A literal sea of green.

Near the Hoh Bridge are massive bars of sand and silt. Buried deeply now is the soil from the earliest residents' upriver farms, which were frequently swept away by uncaring currents. The tales of the trials of the pioneers are nearly unimaginable. The indigenous peoples had for centuries mastered life here by taking what was given. They lived near the sea in closeness with the earth. They ate what was provided. The immigrants knew only farming and raising livestock and could not have chosen a worse place to do so.

The Olympic Peninsula juts defiantly into the Pacific Ocean as if trying to stretch beyond the reach and influence of civilization. Perhaps yearning for a chance to return to untouched wildness. You come to the unique desolation of this rain-sodden land with the knowledge that this region will ever be true to its dramatic natural history.

You must of course take a walk in the woods on your way to or from the top of the peninsula. Choose any of the river roads that take you deep into the rain forest—Quinault, Hoh, Queets, Bogachiel, or Sol Duc. Here you'll feel the power of a most imposing fusion of geology, climate, and surely something more spiritual, more

important. You stand silent in cathedrals of green and try to imagine the harmonic existence of the native peoples as well as the resolve and toughness of the nineteenth century pioneers, each doing what their cultures do best in this unimaginably unforgiving setting.

We begin our roadtrip at the town of Sappho where you leave US 101 and wander north. It's near here on Lake Pleasant that a company of army soldiers formed up a century ago to harvest the spruce wood critical to the fledgling aircraft industry during World War I. The railroad bed they graded along the north shore of Lake Crescent remains as a non-motorized trail. Driving up the winding Burnt Mountain Road—Washington Highway 113—it's hard to imagine that this was once a primary commercial route between the lumber camps and Clallam Bay, the site of a busy shipping port in the late nineteenth century.

Highway 112 is a designated National Scenic Highway, and on a previous visit I had ventured west to the far tip of the country. The Makah Indian Reservation at Neah Bay and the remote

Moss and ferns carpet the rainforest floor

and thoroughly enchanting Lake Ozette with its beautiful beach trails are certainly worth a visit, so be my guest. But today you and I will explore the route back to the east. Follow the Pysht River through Pysht, a quite intriguing name for a nearly imperceptible town, and your first meeting with the Strait of Juan de Fuca at Pillar Point. As you parallel the sea, fingers of fog tease onto the land and make the defiantly curvy drive even more interesting.

Most of what you see around you—if you

dare take your eyes off the wickedly curving road—is the agriculture of trees. Where fur trappers once prowled the deep woods between the strait and the high hills, so-called replacement forests now rule. You won't find anything like civilization until you get to Joyce—nothing but the hills and your ever-turning automobile. Be not afraid, this is a National Scenic Highway—it's supposed to do that.

I arrived at Crescent Bay as the shadows grew long. The easily accessible beach at Salt Creek County Park welcomes you for some stunning sunsets if the conditions favor. Strewn with agates and weathered drift logs, the old pilings rising from the sea grass and displays of mist make for some fine photos and memories. This bay very nearly was the center for shipping and transport as well as the county seat until a failed attempt at a seawall forced the railroad to abort their connection. All that's left is a return to natural beauty and an unrepentant recollection of past enterprise.

The road now leads away from the shore. I looped back once more through Joyce and over the ridge to the north shore of beautiful, breezy Lake Crescent. I was now within the Olympic National Park boundary, and I slowed as a group of hikers walked along the road to take their place among the trees on the lake bank in the lowering sun.

I ended my day aside the Elwah River a bit below the dam at Lake Mills. The clear and slow-swirling water, perfectly warmed in the reservoir, invited me for a quiet swim. Above me, heavy tangles of moss draped an ancient maple like a ragged wool overcoat. Peering off into the deep forest I saw the light greens before me become emerald, turning darker as they went deeper. Then all light was lost, the scene turned black and disappeared into time.

Interesting name, unique place, yet curiously absent from all the guidebooks I haul everywhere I go. If I'm to give you a telling vignette of Joyce, information and inspiration will have to come from more unconventional sources. So I stepped out of the car into the hazy August sun and turned my imagination in the direction of the old depot and then to the well-dressed country store. Hoping for a vision, I took a photo and wandered on.

Much later I am hunched at the computer, ready to abandon fantasy and fabrication for online facts. Behold, The Joyce Community Webpage appears to reconstruct my earlier squint-eyed view of the abandoned village. I give the photo I took another look.

I'm standing along the highway once more, but now I see a jolly man in overalls playing banjo in front of the oldest general store in the state. A mill train is chugging into the West's last log-built depot, screaming steam and spitting smoke. I step quickly out of the way of a purple tissue-trimmed float pulled by an antique tractor. The Wild Blackberry Festival Queen smiles down and waves queen-like as she passes.

Hometowns are always just as you see them, but you gotta know how to look.

Mount Rainier lords over eastern Thurston County

LOCATION:
- Southwest Washington in western Thurston and eastern Grays Harbor Counties
- Benchmark Atlas pages 82, 83
- Loop route from Olympia approximately 60 miles

SIGHTS AND SCENES:
- Olympia, whose capitol in the shadow of the Black Hills overlooks southernmost Puget Sound
- The forested, deforested, and reforested hills above the Chehalis and Black River plains
- Old timber towns, quaint businesses, and riverside hangouts
- Magical Mima prairie and acres of baby Douglas fir trees

FOLLOW ME:
- From Olympia take US 101 west to State Highway 8
- Near McCleary turn south onto Mox-Chehalis Road
- Follow Mox-Chehalis Road to the town of Malone and State Highway 12
- Go southwest through Porter and Oakville then turn left on Moon Road to Gate
- Take Gate Road, then Mima Road across the Black River Valley to Waddell Creek Road
- Return to the Olympia area on Delphi Road

BACKROAD TRIP 2

LOOPING THE BLACK HILLS
Getting Lost for Beginners

Orderly tree farms line the Black River plain

This drive circles the low hills that border the southernmost reaches of Puget Sound. You'll find weary wooden towns, built on small-scale farming and timber, hiding along the wide valleys of Thurston and Grays Harbor Counties.

A classy combination of history and progress, the capital city of

Olympia is nestled along the lower bays of Puget Sound. With convenient access to the mountains, ocean, and Olympic Peninsula, you can venture out in any direction and be immersed in any number of wildly different backroad views and experiences. Today it's your starting point for a trip around those dark forested hills one can see off to the southwest from the broad lawn of the state capitol campus.

From Olympia take U.S. Highway 101 west and then State Highway 8 to McCleary, where you turn south onto the two-lane Mox-Chehalis Road. Curve slowly, following the creek through scenic pastures and forested hillsides, passing barns, old machinery, tattered fences, and houses. The road ends in Malone on Highway 12, and you direct your car southeast along the broad plain of the Chehalis River. Down the highway a few miles you'll find Porter, one of so many retired sawmill towns in the Pacific Northwest. Except for the quaint and historic Porter Creek Inn, the town seems unremarkable—until you explore the backstreets and wander up Porter Creek Road.

Now is a great time to practice some key backroading principles. If you endeavor to make these journeys unforgettable, pay close attention: The joy is in the journey. Avoid observing sameness. Train your weather-proof eyes to see simple beauty, and celebrate the history, style, and glory unique to each scene. Prowl, question, hang out, poke around. Finally, whenever possible, get lost. If you don't know where you are, you've arrived.

As I drove up Porter Creek, I wandered past a weathered porch within a flapping explosion of bright yellow—dizzy dozens of willow goldfinches likely drawn by a thistle-seed feeder. Summer scents—the spice of huckleberry and that heady backroad smell of sweet clover—

swirled up from the valley. On the way out of town, a sparsely toothed old man waved from his stoop and smiled with squinting eyes—an icon in overalls.

Back on the eastbound lane of the highway, you'll soon cruise into Oakville. There you'll find a century-old hardware store with just too much old-time charm to pass by. There must be something you need in there! Batteries for that flashlight long forgotten in the glovebox, perhaps a roll of film, an odd kitchen implement from way up in the attic, or a couple pounds of shiny nails—still sold in bulk barrels. The whole journey would be worth this visit alone for a nostalgic return to what retail used to be.

Just a bit east of Oakville, turn left on Moon Road and you can sneak back to the Olympia area through the back door. The Gate and Mima Roads twist you north, alternately hugging the hillside and skirting the prairie. Near Gate, flat farms are being sprinkled with tract houses slowly spreading up from Rochester and down from Tumwater. A hundred years ago the lower Black River Valley embraced commercial fields of strawberries, hops, and fruit orchards. With fine views of Mount Rainier off to the east, this shift to the new rural economy is understandable if just a tad lamentable.

As you weave through the Black River lowlands, you'll pass Weyerhaeuser tree farms. I gazed over mile after flat square mile of Doug fir seedling sprouts carpeting the scenery. In the distant backdrop of the Capitol State Forest, shaved hills prepare to welcome these well-groomed offspring and another new forest. I continue north past the Littlerock turnoff, up Waddell Creek Road, and into some very curious landscaping.

Mima Mounds Natural Area Preserve is a strange and popular geological roadside attraction. Drop into the interpretive area and try to solve the mysterious origin of these hilly phenomena. Glacial ice floes, giant gopher hills, or cosmic goose bumps? You be the judge.

From the Mima prairie you have two choices. You can return to Littlerock then proceed north to Tumwater on the Littlerock Road, or continue

Sailing on Puget Sound near Olympia

to straddle the Capitol State Forest on the Waddell Creek Road on through the Delphi Valley and back to the west side of Olympia. Both offer a pleasant reentry.

This comfortable drive can be done easily in a half day. Load up the family, call a friend, or go it alone. Brush up on your local history and carry a good map. Be ready to wander off a bit, and to shift gears at anytime. A good roadtrip is an art form, and the open road is your canvas. Express yourself!

• Hometown •
McCLEARY

The old door factory is still in business. The yard lights, the hum, and the smell of sawdust on the rain assure you that this will always be a mill town. But the glory days are surely gone. Gone with the old growth, and the plywood factory, and the wealth, and the time when Simpson owned and operated the entire city—owned the houses, operated the banks, and ran the government. There's something purposeful and certain about company towns. Doing it their way.

I occasionally have business in town and recently dropped into the local tavern to carry out some small-town research. Come to find out that Dan is still running the place. I had met him decades ago in the urban cowboy years singing with his band up in the big city. This is his tavern, his town. You'll find him sitting in with the boys that perform here on the weekends, still expertly singing the classic country hits. Does flawless Cash and nails Haggard.

McCleary comes here out of the rain and smiles for a few hours on Saturday night. Dan's taking care of folks, seeing they have someplace to be, putting a roof over their heads, and cashing their checks. Purposeful and certain. Doing it his way.

A lone trawler seeks the shelter of the jetty

LOCATION:

- Southwest Washington in Pacific, Wahkiakum and Cowlitz Counties
- Benchmark Atlas pages 95, 96
- Route from Stella to the Long Beach Peninsula with a visit to Puget Island approximately 78 miles

SIGHTS AND SCENES:

- Quaint villages and hidden backwaters served by magical backroads
- Ocean mists and transport ships that roll with you along the Columbia River
- Weathered buildings, cranberry bogs, broken trawlers in back yards, and a covered bridge, all set in a wet and gray unreality
- Long Beach, home to big-time salmon fishing, bay oysters, sand sculptures, and kite flying

FOLLOW ME:

- Begin at Stella on Washington Highway 4 and motor west to Cathlamet
- Cross the bridge to Puget Island and circle the island on Birnie, Cross Island, and Sunny Sands Roads
- From Cathlamet to Skamokawa follow the cut-off through the deer refuge on Steamboat Slough Road
- At Skamokawa take side trips up Middle Valley and Wilson Creek Roads for a different view of things
- Continue on Washington 4 through Grays River. Take a shortcut on Covered Bridge Road
- About 11 miles west of Grays River choose your path to the sea: Highway 4 to US Highway 101 via Willapa Bay, or Highway 401 with a return to the Columbia River and a connection with 101 at Megler
- From Ilwaco and Long Beach prowl the peninsula to your heart's delight

BAYOU COUNTRY

Mists and Mystery along Highway 4

The North Head lighthouse near Ilwaco

Most all that remained of Stella when I was here years ago was the old tavern. A classic roadhouse perched on pilings met you at the river once you escaped from the interstate back in Longview. Poised on the shore, it welcomed you to 150 years of life on the river. Stella had disappeared twice during its life as a booming riverport, destroyed by fire. I didn't notice the old Stella Tavern as I passed this foggy day. Either it was there or it wasn't. I enjoyed the thought of mystical uncertainty accompanying my trip into the haze and magic of the river's mouth. The frequent mists, rain, and fog that live along the Lower Columbia can transform the scenes and structures into something make-believe.

Westbound Highway 4 escorts you to this world away as you hug the shore. Big old river on one side, rolling forested hills on the other. At Cathlamet in tiny Wahkiakum County, wander the dozen quaint city blocks on the slope above the Columbia. The region's past is displayed at an inauspicious historical museum on the backside of town. The story of the Lower Columbia goes something like this: Pioneers arrived in the mid-1800s, placed pilings in the rivers and camps in the forests, sent away the logs in rafts and salmon in cans, and then followed them away to who knows where. Perhaps that is oversimplified and abrupt, but you get the picture.

From the Cathlamet waterfront a bridge leads to Puget Island. I dropped in just to see what happens on an island in the middle of the West's largest river. The fog had cleared and revealed dairy farm flatness and unmistakable island self-sufficiency. Puget Island serves as a stepping stone to the Oregon side should you be headed that way. In crossing the south channel you will take the last operating ferryboat on the lower Columbia.

Ten miles west of Cathlamet, immense freighters glide past Skamokawa Vista Park so close you can touch them from the shore. In hollows nearby, curious collections of rural esoterica hunker down—rusting pieces of small lumber mills, old car carcasses, a Baptist Mission housed in a sagging and mossy trailer. I spent a couple hours wandering the poorly marked backroads that weave along the bayous. Most call them sloughs, but that is nowhere near as mysterious

or romantic. A peek through the backwater damp reveals ramshackle houseboats bridled to ancient moorings.

Beyond Skamokawa, Highway 4 eases inland, leaving behind riverside miles dotted with sturgeon fishermen stretched over the guardrails with ten-foot fiberglass poles. What is it like when they catch one? The image of an eight-foot-long prehistoric fish writhing on the shoulder of the road certainly added to the fantasy.

Continuing west, the covered bridge at Grays River can be found near the town of the same

Bales of shells guard a commercial oyster plant

name. Naselle is one of the bigger smaller towns in these parts. If the drive has you hungry, you may be able to score an oysterburger or some clam strips with hot sauce.

At this point you have two choices, as both Highways 401 and 4 will take you to Ilwaco and the mouth of the Columbia. Both these alternatives are worthy. Veering south on 401 returns you to the river and that sense of bigness. Along

here you can smell the damp air turn saltier as you drive west where the Astoria Bridge spans your horizon—four miles shore to shore. Or you might follow the Naselle River to its mouth at Willapa Bay, one of the country's most unspoiled estuaries. As you near the beach, look for soggy acres of cranberry bogs laying low in the fog. There is much to see and do in Long Beach, Ilwaco, and Seaview. Slowly drive up the peninsula to Nahcotta and Oysterville because there's nothing like what you'll see. A railroad used to run this route and would occasionally get stuck in the sand. Don't let this happen to you.

I love these beachside communities! I am in awe of the countless ways the keepers of all the weathered-chic cottages have found to decorate their eaves, porches, and falling-down fences with washed up beach treasures!

Here is more high praise for the Washington coast—it is the foremost year-round roadtrip destination. December or July, it's pretty much the same. Bayous and beaches hold their own in the surrealness of the drizzle and fog of winter as well as the hushed sun of summer.

There is no risk of mistaking the lower Columbia as anywhere else. The scenes enriched with river haze and ocean fog are just uncertain enough to pleasantly skew reality. Your visit to the bayous and beaches is only as factual as the imagination allows.

● Hometown ●
OYSTERVILLE

It's only a healthy walk across the peninsula from the straight and sandy beach where the breakers boom to the sheltered edge of Willapa Bay with its curves and mudflats. The long, narrow neighborhood of Long Beach stretches from Seaview to Oysterville to Leadbetter Point and is beautifully strewn with small storm-seasoned summer rentals and their white-shelled driveways. Oysterville is very curious and salty, outwardly rugged, and inwardly delicate and rich, perhaps even sensuous. Just like the oyster itself. I reloaded my camera and silently wondered how many years one must spend in Writer's Purgatory for such a frantic metaphor. But I pressed on.

Precious native oysters once spread across the tidelands; rare nuggets soon depleted by enterprising pilgrims. These miners stayed on, the bays were reseeded, and soon vacationers rolled in like the fog. All are now part of the rare delicacy of the peninsula itself. They stay for the sweet and deep taste, so easy and abundant, best enjoyed in its rawness.

By now I was convinced the muse of lame imagery hovered nearby and was writing me up! Fine. I sat on a damp beach log with a screwdriver and a leather glove, a small bucket of raw ones in the shell, and cold can of beer. Practicing as I preach.

Flatland fields near Conway in early spring

20

LOCATION:
- Northwest Washington in western Skagit and Whatcom Counties
- Benchmark Atlas page 42
- Loop route beginning near Mt. Vernon approximately 115 miles

SIGHTS AND SCENES:
- Curvy Chuckanut Drive hugging the hillside above Bellingham Bay
- The shops, eateries, and Victorian homes of funky Fairhaven
- Pioneer Dutch Lynden with what looks like a real windmill
- Nooksack, Everson, Deming, and Sedro-Woolley —calm valley towns born of the logging boom
- Backyards, barnyards, graveyards, and dairylands

FOLLOW ME:
- From Mount Vernon go north on Interstate 5 to the Chuckanut Drive Exit
- Head northwest across Samish Flats on Highway 11 to Fairhaven
- Turn right on Valley Parkway to return to I-5 north
- Exit at Guide-Meridian Avenue (Highway 539)
- Go north to Front Street, turn right and into Lynden
- Take Hampton, Van Buren, and Tom Roads to Highway 9 and Nooksack
- Follow Highway 9 south to Sedro-Woolley
- Proceed west on Cook Road to return to Interstate 5

NORTHWEST PASSAGES
Chuckanut, Nooksack, and Back

BACKROAD TRIP 4

Abandoned rail trestle in Skagit County

If there would be just one symbol of roadtripping in Washington, it would surely be the 25-mile stretch of backroad named Chuckanut Drive. Though any marginally astute engineer would tell you Washington Highway 11 should long ago have stumbled off the side of Chuckanut Mountain and into Bellingham Bay,

it hangs there still as the ultimate freeway bypass and must-see side trip.

Welcome to Whatcom and Skagit Counties. On this diverse roadtrip you'll explore an interesting balance of geography, scenery, industry, and the forces that play between rural and residential.

In younger days I frequently fled Seattle and headed north. My old pickup truck Angelo and I used to break free of the metropolitan chatter once we escaped Everett; now the urban crawl chases you up I-5 as far as the town of Mount Vernon. Just beyond this trendy and tulip-trimmed tourist stop, Highway 11 breaks away on Exit 231. The narrow two-lane veers northwest in a keen slice across the Samish Flats. This moist and rich bottomland became home to the farming know-how brought by European pioneers over a century ago. The buffet table is set with corn, peas, milk, oysters, and everything in between along eight short miles. July roadside ditches frame your route in fireweed and daisies. If the westerly winds are fair, you may spot a hang glider or two launching from the top of Chuckanut Mountain.

After completing your twisty cruise along Chuckanut Drive sneaking peeks at the San Juan Islands to your left, Bellingham's historic Fairhaven District calls you in. Get out and stretch, wander down along the harborside path and smell the roses. Bellingham is actually a collection of four towns that merged their mismatched street plans and common dreams way back when. Though worthy, we'll bypass the center of town for now to seek a more dispersed and distinctive type of charm.

Return to the I-5 freeway heading north, and at Exit 256 slide onto the Guide Meridian Road toward Lynden. Once again that good old "getting out of the city" feeling takes over! You hit

the inland flatlands and cruise that fuzzy line between postmodern development and the inability of "the good old days" to keep up: deserted drive-in theater and rusty wrecking yard meet Blockbuster Video and Schuck's Auto Supply. Lynden lies half way to Canada and out

Bulb farms show spring color

on its own. Lynden grounds you, gives you hope, inspires you, and is a story in itself. Imagine a planet with more bakeries than beer joints! Visit the Pioneer Museum and grab a bite at any one of many quaint cafes; then you're ready to enter the shady backside of our route.

You drop away from Lynden on Hampton Road and hit the bottomland, long cleared of trees and reclaimed from the Nooksak River by dikes, dynamite, and dairies. When you get to Highway 9 turn south to Deming, a town with a rich forest history and a near-world-class logging show each spring to prove it. A bit farther south, beyond the Highway 9/542 junction, I stopped to grab a double box of fresh raspberries from

an unattended roadside card table. I made a big deal of dropping my three dollars in the old baking soda can since I was being closely watched from all the cars lining up behind my car, which was idling in the middle of the road.

Three miles down the valley—it's becoming more wooded out now—you can pull over and pay your respects at the Case-Nooksack Cemetery, which sits on a rise by the side of the highway. A most weird and eclectic collection of devices and icons decorate the graves. From the standard Madonna—looking a tad sad in this lonely place—to pink flamingoes. There's a tangle of faded plastic flowers. Is that a ceramic deer? Next to one tilted headstone is some graven idol made from tin, wire, and rubber bands. Eerie backroad artistry never fails to please.

You're on your own the rest of the way. If you tend to be thrilled by tree farms, yards filled with rusting cars, and towns with names like Acme, Clipper, and Wickersham, you don't need my help. It's about 22 miles from Deming to Sedro-Woolley, which was once the edge of the known world to Puget Sounders. Now it seems all of a block away from the hustle and haste. Not ready to join in? Jump on Cook Road, head west back to the flats, and drift awhile. You'll get home eventually.

A view of Rainier from the Green River Valley

24

LOCATION:

- Central Puget Sound area in Eastern King County
- Benchmark Atlas pages 70, 71, 84, 85
- Roundtrip route from Maple Valley approximately 43 miles

SIGHTS AND SCENES:

- A shortcut over the Cascades if you're real lucky, the Green River Waterworks Gate if not
- Once-tiny and bucolic burgs scattered about the Green and Cedar Rivers
- 150 years of the history of Puget Sound industry and development—a big dose in a small area
- Clean woodsy riverside escapes to break from the crowds

FOLLOW ME:

- Begin in Maple Valley and drive south on Highway 18 to the Kent-Kangley Road (Highway 516)
- Left on Hwy 516 toward Georgetown with a detour through Ravensdale
- Right on the Retreat-Kanaskat Road to Kanaskat, then Palmer
- From the town of Palmer you may wish to drive up the Green River and ask to go to Lester at the Waterworks Gate
- Failing that, prowl up the Kanaskat-Selleck Road to Selleck
- Backtrack south to Cumberland and follow the Green River Gorge Road to Black Diamond
- Return to Maple Valley on Highway 169

BACKROAD TRIP 5

STAMPEDE PASS IMPASSE

Confusion in the Foothills

Fall colors trim an east King County backroad

There are lots of fine and popular backroad journeys within easy driving distance of Seattle. That's what happens when you drop a huge city between two mountain ranges and an inlet of the sea. If you are visiting the Seattle/Tacoma/Everett area, your rental car or your in-law's minivan can take

you down well-known roads to picture-book destinations.

But sometimes it's darn hard to get off the beaten path! Sometimes it turns out that The Road Less Traveled is that way for a reason. Fortunately for you, this backroad explorer takes the dares, studies the maps, and chases down the dead ends so you won't have to! Such it was a couple years back as I determined to drive up the Green River and across Stampede Pass.

It took me more than two hours of wandering around to learn that the road over Stampede from Palmer to Easton is not open to the public. I'm still baffled why I didn't know that prior to my drive into eastern King County. Maybe I should have called ahead.

I set out toward Kanaskat and began my search for the Stampede Pass Road and the old railroad town of Lester. Following miles of gender-appro-priate resistance to asking directions, I drove an unmarked road to the Green River Waterworks office and winked at the smiling young lady at the desk. I asked that she kindly issue me a permit so I might pass through the big gate onto Forest Road 54 and follow the railroad up and over the Cascade crest to Stampede and on to eastern Washington. Just as a favor. Just this one time.

A gruff and seasoned voice hiding behind a file cabinet answered for her, "Why would we want to do that?!"

Briefly startled, I replied, "Well, I could pay you, I guess." I thought I might swing a deal with the invisible man.

"Not likely." He'd heard it all before.

"I work for the government," I lied.

"Whose?" he asked. He was still just a talking file cabinet.

"OK, I'm a writer. I'm doing a story on all the nice people who work up this valley."

"Talk to the main office in Seattle. And if you haven't noticed, I'm not that nice."

"I just want to pass through, that's all."

The young woman just smiled silently.

"Look," he said, "this area has been closed to recreational use for thirty years. If we let one guy through, we'd have to let them all through. Before you know it, the area would be filled with noise, people would make their own roads, the streams would have mud in them, fish runs would be ruined, and the hills would be dusty, unsightly, and littered."

An old tractor hides in a lonely backlot

"So who can go in there?" I asked, though I knew the ironic answer.

"Logging trucks," he said, "Just logging trucks."

In retreat, lesson learned, I returned to the lowlands to get a grip on the old and the new that were scattered about this former coal mining and logging region.

Any and all of the small towns rimming the west slope of the Cascades in eastern King County are worth wheeling through—they are such a stark departure from Seattle, the country's eighteenth largest city and among the most automobility challenged.

The map suggests a route that will even get you off the once-lonely roads that now are prowled by SUVs taking the better-off city folk to their wooded suburban homes. Ravensdale is as backwoods as you please, and the old store in Palmer will delight the curio shopper. Black Diamond has a too-tempting bakery near a wonderfully cluttered logging and history museum that speaks to the upbringing of the entire area. The rest is patchy forests and fields and the landscape interface of civilization scraping away at rural America.

I spent the late afternoon at Kanaskat-Palmer Park where the Green River beautifully thunders and twists, its source somewhere in that mysterious land up Stampede Pass never to be seen.

There may yet be an honest way into the Green River Watershed. My days of jumping a Union Pacific freight or mountain biking forty-five miles are well behind me. I'm open to suggestions, so give it a try. Maybe you can fall in line with the local Jeep club—these guys know how to backroad the backroads. When you get to Lester you be sure and let me know.

• Hometown •
RAVENSDALE

I was lost in a vortex of roads. Some retained their lyrical and logical country names, and some sported new signs marking three-digit-southwest. Around the corner from the old gun club, a tightly packed row of seventy-year-old houses fronted the shabby two-lane road. Nearby in the morning fog, an asphalt blender churned out a wider way into and out of town. In two hours it would reach the gated development that was pushed back against a no longer forested hill.

I recalled when this was truly the sticks—screeching train whistles, very old pickups, and a day-long row of Harleys in front of the tavern. But progress comes, and I suppose that even the roughest railroad town is destined to soften at the edges. Having had my reflective moment, I ceremoniously set my opinions down on the old road. By later this afternoon they, too, would be paved over and all would be well.

Lucia Falls on the East Fork of the Lewis River

28

LOCATION:
- *Southwest Washington in Clark County between the Columbia River and the Cascade foothills*
- *Benchmark Atlas pages 109, 110*
- *Loop route from Woodland with a side trip to Ridgefield approximately 86 miles*

SIGHTS AND SCENES:
- *A patchwork of cute-sounding towns folded into green ravines*
- *Monuments to the pioneer past: gristmills, saw mills, orchards, and an old-time railroad*
- *A world-class swimming hole along one of many roads that head for the hills and beyond*
- *Totally unique Ridgefield, which rests above the Columbia shore*

FOLLOW ME:
- *From the town of Woodland on Interstate 5, go east on the Lewis River Road (Highway 503) through Ariel and Yale*
- *After 23 miles, 503 heads south and you'll pass through Chelatchie then Amboy, where you'll find the Amboy Road into Yacolt*
- *Follow the railroad to the East Fork of the Lewis River and Moulton Falls Park then back to Lucia Falls and the town of Lucia*
- *Take Basket Flats Road through Heisson*
- *Follow NE 142nd south to Battle Ground*
- *Return north on Highway 503 to Fargher Lake*
- *West on 379th to NE 94th to Lockwood Road gets you to La Center*
- *Cross the Interstate on La Center Road and choose your route out to and around Ridgefield*

LEWIS RIVER RAMBLING
Shower Power in "River County"

Summer in rural Lewis County

Through a roadside break in the rain-laden forest I peeked in on the Lewis River, steely gray-green and swollen with the spring weather. This trip would politely refute the notion that roadtrips are only for sunny afternoons. Another spring shower boomed down, brief but accurate, leaving foothill forests steeped in lime-colored leaves and moss-muffled trunks. Roadside slopes wave towers of purple foxgloves, fearless sword ferns, and tangles of daisies.

This loop through the flatlands and foothills east of the Columbia River can be done in an afternoon; it's all within striking distance of Vancouver, one of the state's larger cities. I have marked out the route I chose that wet spring day, but what you want to do is ditch the freeway and start careening around. A road here, a road there. Put your map on the dash, pick a town, and when you find it head for the next.

This region has a prominent place in Northwest history. Fort Vancouver was the center of British trade and industry in the early nineteenth century and welcomed settlers from every part of the world. Old orchards, gristmills, logging roads, grange buildings, and churches relate the hard life of settlement. The foothill pageant of rivers and rain, rails and roads surrounds as you prowl through this pictorial.

I exited Interstate 5 at Woodland and pointed east, passed the Oddfellow Cemetery, and turned onto Highway 503 up the north shore of the Lewis River. Past Lake Merwin the route turns south and twists impossibly below Yale Dam to a series of quaint and quiet prairies that host towns whose history is farming and timber.

Amboy is buried in the deep, wet green of spring and huddled around Chelatchie Creek, which once powered a mighty mill wheel. Take the back road to Yacolt to where the old-time railroad still runs. Follow the tracks south to join the East Fork of the Lewis River.

Along the road in a field of pink-tinged timothy grass stands a sign that reads: I want to live in River County! This secessionist sentiment is found in the foothill half of every county from here to Canada and tells me I'm nearing the (real

or imagined) zoning designations between "rural/bucolic" and "gentrified/sprawling."

On hotter days, the East Fork's Moulton Falls hosts teeming crowds of youngsters crashing into cool pools from atop house-high boulders. The town of Battle Ground continues to deal with uncertainty. Bad enough to be named after a battle that never occurred, now it must wonder if it

is more grange hall or mega market, proud pioneer legacy or low-country tract house—"River County" or Clark County.

I pushed on in the rain, taking the straight and narrow Highway 503 north to Fargher Lake; I then pointed west on a series of more imaginative backroads to return to Woodland. Alongside Fargher Pond, an immense and aging workshed spoke at length about life in the early 1900s. It was framed and floored with beams the size of rail ties. Inside dozed a dust-faded thresher and an equally ancient bailer. A matched set.

To get the full effect of this region, find your way across Interstate 5 and prowl the off-by-itself hamlet of Ridgefield. A small town not yet given to the ways of today, it sits surrounded by powerful examples of pioneer history. The migration of white settlers flowed from the south, and folks were quick to settle here. Early industry included dried fruit, granite paving stone from a nearby quarry, wheat, and dairy products. The remnants of orchards, worksites, and pioneer houses dot the roads that roll in and out of this town on the Columbia riverbank. The nearby wildlife refuge is the temporary home of a quarter-million waterfowl each year.

As I returned to the freeway and headed home, the rain was easing and the June-high sun flowed onto the greening fields. Vegetation was at full-throttle. I paused to photograph a blackberry bush leaning its ball bat–thick stem against a tired old shed wall. Some sunny day I plan to return to see if this old weathered structure survives without being devoured by spring's green explosion.

Cedar and vine maple thrive on frequent foothill rains

● Hometown ●
YACOLT

A large crowd of teenagers played on the wooden train platform, waiting out the final days of summer vacation. Taunting and teasing, posturing and posing—stretching hard toward grownup ways, of which they could only guess. A student of nature, I sat on a curb on the unbusy street and observed the dance of this timeless social behavior.

The railroad landing served the tourist train that came and went between here and Moulton Falls. You can drive to Yacolt and for a few bucks treat the family to a trip through the forest to the outback and back. The season was now winding down and the tracks were pressed into duty as balance beams for teenage showoffs.

The group gradually was selected away, and after awhile only the tallest, best-looking boy remained with what I supposed to be the most popular girl. The others raced around and grouped and paired then split up and soon scattered to other parts of this town that didn't appear to have many other parts.

The king and queen of the platform stood in awkward silence, looking down the tracks. As I watched them I imagined they both were hoping the train would come and take them far away from small-town life to some magic land on the other side of the woods.

Old Thorpe Mill on the banks of the Yakima River

LOCATION:
- Central Washington in western Kittitas County
- Benchmark Atlas pages 86, 87
- Roundtrip route from Roslyn to Ellensburg and back approximately 48 miles

SIGHTS AND SCENES:
- The historic and eccentric coal mining hilltown of Roslyn
- The riverside meandering of former cross-state Highway 10
- Old Ellensburg's story-telling backstreets, rail depot, and rodeo grounds
- Fragrant valley grasslands and a timeless restored flour mill near Thorpe

FOLLOW ME:
- To get to Roslyn take eastbound Interstate 5 exit 80
- From Roslyn go downhill on Washington Highway 903 into Cle Elum
- Jog a block in Cle Elum to go east on Highway 907
- 3 miles out of town merge onto State Highway 10
- After 7 or so miles take a right onto Thorp Road, cross the river, and explore the valley
- Return to Hwy 10 or cross the freeway and follow the signs into Ellensburg
- After exploring Ellensburg, go north on "A" Street then west on W. 15th Avenue, which becomes Dry Creek Road and takes you to Highway 97 north
- Proceed 13 miles northwest on 97 and then left on 970, which will return you to Cle Elum and Roslyn

THE UPPER YAKIMA

BACKROAD TRIP 7

From Hilltown to Heartland

Heading downriver on old Highway 10

How about a first taste of the dry side of the mountains? This trip is only a couple of hours from the Puget Sound clatter and takes you from piney hills to riparian grasslands, through towns big on character and short on people.

The drive begins in the historic and eclectic town of Roslyn.

Take a moment to locate The Brick Tavern, a good spot to relax after the journey. It is said the TV series Northern Exposure put Roslyn on the map, but that's not quite true. Long before the quirky scripts and media attention appeared, there were once-booming coal mines, assorted cemeteries with picturesque grave-stones, an open doorway to mountain trails and lakes, and the annual Manly Man Festival and Spam cook-off.

Take the highway downhill and through Cle Elum, a place somehow making the unearthly leap from dying lumber town to Seattle suburb. A few miles east of Cle Elum on State Road 970, locate Highway 10—the old cross-state road—and two-lane it along the Yakima River. This superb stretch of backroad flows and turns with the stream and adjoining railroad tracks. Rugged rock canyon walls frame the peaceful drive. Across the river you'll see the abandoned Milwaukee Pacific railbed that is now part of the John Wayne Trail, the state's longest hiking, biking, and equestrian path, stretching all the way to Idaho. And over-head you'll spot remnants of old irrigation flumes that once fed the thirsty valley downstream.

Halfway to Ellensburg, turn right on the Thorp Road and enter the river plain below. In the warm stillness you can reflect on what it was like a century ago when settlers farmed this area. Ahead, the recently restored Thorp Mill sits proudly by the river. In days past, the large stone wheel produced flour for the homesteaders and meal for their teams, which pulled wagons of folks roadtripping from the valley settlements of Kittitas, Taneum, and Teanaway.

If you have them, it's time to unfasten your bicycles from the car rack and explore the valley. Two-wheel or slowly drive the nearby farm roads, windows down, amid the heavy perfume of sage, pine, and river willow. If you arrive in June, the scent of flowering locust trees will have you smiling; the spring redolence is heady and crowded on the warm wind.

I pulled over and sat on the riverbank under the Thorp Bridge and watched rafts and drift boats parade by with faceless sportsmen wearing caps and sunglasses. Silently entering stage left, they plinked and swirled in the rills and eddies then disappeared around the bend to the right. I felt like I was in some sort of surreal "Trout Fishing in America" diorama. The Yakima is among the most popular streams in the state to cast a fly. Try your luck.

A short drive to the east, Ellensburg hides its charms well. Looping down the side streets along the tracks reveals the enduring brick backsides of a once-thriving commerce. Along this urban backroad you'll notice tipsy ninety-year-old work-sheds and tatty lots of abandoned and obscure machinery. Downtown hosts some great old-time eateries and a couple of the state's coolest thrift stores. Spin around Ellensburg, passing the aged railroad station and up to the old rodeo grounds. Though likely vacant now, it'll be raucous with hoofed mayhem come Labor Day.

An option for the return drive takes you north on Highway 97, then back to Cle Elum by way of Hwy 970. The 97/970 junction is the gateway to Blewitt Pass and the sky-stabbing Stuart Range that has been grabbing your gaze all along your journey through the lowlands.

Your stool awaits above the spittin' trough at The Brick if you make it back to Roslyn. A rewarding alternative would be the T&E Tavern in Thorp. Truly a four-star roadtrip roadhouse! Seated at the large window you can nibble free peanuts and watch the emerald valley at its summer's work—day by day spinning the green fields into gold.

Afternoon moonrise in Kittitas County

• Hometown •
ROSLYN

The Old Number Three Mine was several miles long and stretched under the river and all the way to South Cle Elum. In its day it was one of the most productive coal tunnels in the country. The hillsides and intriguing buildings of Roslyn give you a feel for specialness, but the real story is very much underground. The families that built Roslyn now rest in peace on the edge of town, sorted out by the many ethnic groups or fraternal affiliations that gave each newcomer identity and community.

The mines closed in 1963. In 1976 Roslyn appointed the first black mayor in Washington history—a history that began with statehood in 1889, the same year a train carrying one hundred black miners from Virginia and North Carolina arrived in town to break the striking union that had shut down the mines. Imagine. You can almost feel the coal-fired heat.

Hard work, dirty work, dust, dynamite, union strife, racial unrest, and distance from more modern society. There was nothing soft and easy about living in these rich hills a hundred years ago. The needs of survival and family eventually brought cooperation and peace. Strength of will and hunger for harmony are buried deep, like the remains of the coal that brought them all together.

A winter look at Mount Rainier and the White River from near Crystal Pass

LOCATION:
- The Central Cascades in Pierce and Yakima Counties
- Benchmark Atlas pages 84, 85, 86, 87, 101
- Route from Chinook Pass summit to Yakima with sidetrip to Cowiche and Tieton and back to Naches approximately 86 miles

SIGHTS AND SCENES:
- Mount Rainier, close enough to touch
- Surrounding peaks and passes, abundant hiking, camping, and riverwalking
- The thrill of crossing over to the "warm side" on an overcast western Washington day
- The hilly charms and fruit stands of Naches, Tieton, and Cowiche

FOLLOW ME:
- From the Puget Sound area reach Chinook Pass via Washington Highway 410
- At the summit continue on 410 all the way to Yakima
- From downtown Yakima follow Summitview Avenue into the hills to Cowiche and Tieton
- Return to Naches on Naches-Tieton Road
- From the junction 3 miles west of Naches, choose your return route over the Cascades: Highway 410/Chinook Pass or Washington Highway 12 and White Pass

ACROSS THE DIVIDE
In Search of a Certain Justice

The colorful bounty of the Yakima Valley

Chinook Pass—Washington Highway 410—is surely the grandest drive over the Cascade range. You're welcome to disagree, but I'm afraid you'd be wrong. You see, the North Cascades Highway has its fine scenic moments, and Snoqualmie, White, and Stevens have their comfort, safety, and amenities. But that slow

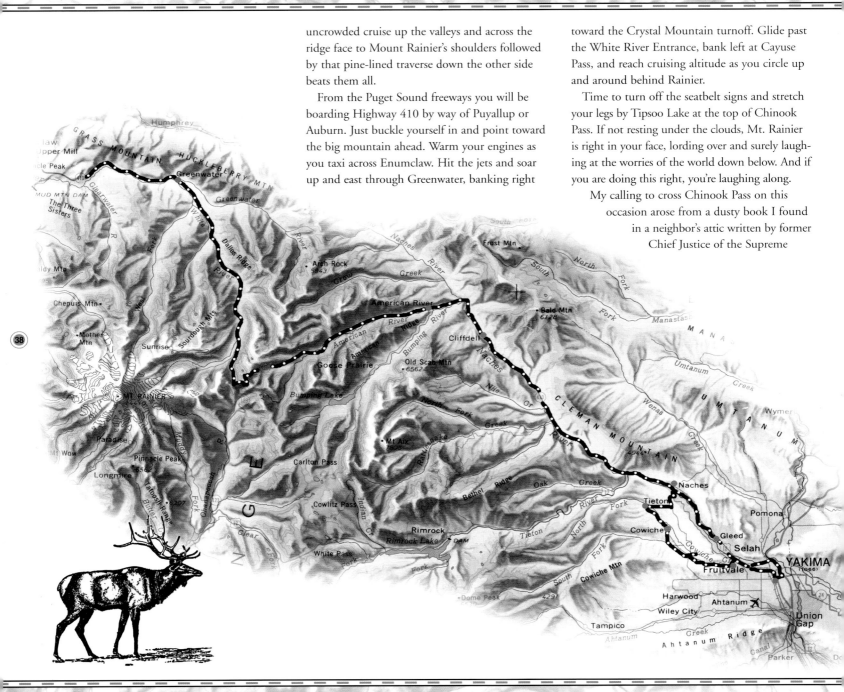

uncrowded cruise up the valleys and across the ridge face to Mount Rainier's shoulders followed by that pine-lined traverse down the other side beats them all.

From the Puget Sound freeways you will be boarding Highway 410 by way of Puyallup or Auburn. Just buckle yourself in and point toward the big mountain ahead. Warm your engines as you taxi across Enumclaw. Hit the jets and soar up and east through Greenwater, banking right toward the Crystal Mountain turnoff. Glide past the White River Entrance, bank left at Cayuse Pass, and reach cruising altitude as you circle up and around behind Rainier.

Time to turn off the seatbelt signs and stretch your legs by Tipsoo Lake at the top of Chinook Pass. If not resting under the clouds, Mt. Rainier is right in your face, lording over and surely laughing at the worries of the world down below. And if you are doing this right, you're laughing along.

My calling to cross Chinook Pass on this occasion arose from a dusty book I found in a neighbor's attic written by former Chief Justice of the Supreme

Court William O. Douglas. In *Of Men and Mountains*, Douglas, who was raised in Yakima, reveals his true gift with words and opinions as he recounts his explorations of the territory east and south of Mt. Rainier in the first half of the twentieth century. He and his young friends would take primitive roads and sheep trails up the river valleys that led to what is still some of the most beautiful alpine scenery on the continent. His honor crossed Chinook, Cowlitz, Cayuse, and Crystal Passes when they were little more than paths and scrambles. His descriptions of the wilds and enchantment with nature are contagious and draw one to see and touch the land he so eloquently describes.

If the great mountain is cloud-bound on your arrival at the Chinook summit, turn your back on the west and ease on down into the land of men and mountains. The forested east slope holds countless trails, peaks, and lonely riversides where you can connect with the land that Douglas loved so much.

Chinook Pass lowers to the basalt canyons below and the green warms to gold. In the summer you will usually experience a 10- to 20-degree increase in temperature between Seattle and south-central Washington. Enter Yakima on Highway 410/12 and take care of any business you might have while looking around at shady parks, cultural color, wineries, walking trails, and fruit markets.

For a truly fine sidetrip that points you home, follow Summitview Avenue up the Cowiche Valley to the so-called Highlands. Fine homes, air conditioners chugging, repose amid orderly orchards. Railroad served this region before the roads were built, and boxcars brought the fruit to market. A walk down the trail on the abandoned rail corridor along the cottonwood-shaded Cowiche Canyon is a nice diversion from driving. Watch out for rattlesnakes.

From the town of Cowiche you can rejoin Highway 12 by passing through Tieton and dropping over the ridge and down to Naches. This is your last chance to shop the roadside stands with local fruits and vegetables for the dinner table at home.

Heading west, I often opt to veer left at the "Y" and on to White Pass for a change of pace, but you certainly can return the way you came. As you once again cross the Chinook Pass summit, consider how young Bill Douglas and his pals would hike from daybreak just to camp up here with the bears and cougars. It must have felt grand to return home with their stories of discovery and the glory of nature's unsubtle beauty. Some things, dare I say, nicely remain the same.

Running Springs Farm near Tieton

• Hometown •
NACHES

You don't learn anything if you don't ask. Last summer on a perfect morning I was stalking the Naches Farmer Fruitstand with camera and curiosity. I knew nature was responsible for the brilliant color on the orderly shelves that drew my lens, but I was sure the story did not end there. Backing up, I knocked a large tomato to the floor—a great way to get the conversation rolling.

Michelle tells me she and her mother, Mary Lou, have arrived here at dawn for years, bringing fruit and produce from the farm down the valley in Zillah. I ask about the many other vendors along the highway and am politely told they really don't have time to go visit other stands. But it didn't prevent mom from sharing her point of view on how many times one should pick apricots in a season (7), unlike some others (2). Or that a melon that reaches its full natural sweetness will never have a stem attached.

I borrowed one of their black marking pens and made notes for this story on the skin of a cantaloupe. I bought some peaches and corn, and gathered my dented tomato and scribbled melon, capped the lens, and retreated up the pass.

Colorful trees trim the walls of Oak Creek Canyon

LOCATION:
- South central Washington in Klickitat County
- Benchmark Atlas pages 112, 113
- A long loop from Maryhill through Klickitat Canyon, over to Bickleton and back, approximately 143 miles

SIGHTS AND SCENES:
- Smooth hills and deep canyons that fold down into the Columbia
- The auspicious Maryhill Museum and illogical Stonehenge set high on the windy gorge walls
- The Columbia Hill benchlands, where small towns and old barns rest before a silhouette of Mt. Adams
- The idyllic and isolated little town of Bickleton

FOLLOW ME:
- Begin at Maryhill on Washington Highway 14
- Drive west about 26 miles along the river to Lyle
- Go north on WA 142 up the Klickitat River and across the benchlands to Goldendale
- Take the Goldendale-Bickleton Highway to Bickleton, approximately 35 miles
- From Bickleton backtrack to the Rock Creek Road and then down the canyon to the Columbia River
- Drive west about 16 miles to return to Maryhill

BACKROAD TRIP
9

THE COLUMBIA GORGE
Where All Backroads Begin

The old ice plant near Klickitat

Beautifully uncluttered Washington Highway 14, along the Columbia River's north bank, is at the top of the list of Washington scenic drives. The captivating vistas of the Columbia Gorge National Scenic Area may also be viewed from Oregon's heavily traveled Interstate 84, but I strongly recommend you do your breathtaking with the easier pace along the Washington shore.

If you begin where U.S. Highway 97 intersects State Highway 14, you can visit the Maryhill Museum of Art and Stonehenge replica. Go ahead, everyone does. What can be learned here, however, transcends the art and history displays. Appreciation of the storied contributions of Mr. Samuel Hill, who brought about the construction of both attractions, is required study for the proficient Washington backroader.

Mr. Hill was renowned as an eccentric, a fearless dreamer, and, importantly, a man with a deep passion for the coming age of automobiles. This man, fellow wanderers, spent a sizable fortune and great effort in the cause of championing paved roads. Remnants of his experiments with various surfacing materials can still be seen on the hillsides above. His advocacy advanced the construction of a highway down the

Columbia Gorge—on the Oregon side—employing innovative techniques to preserve and blend with the natural features along the route.

Hill also envisioned a utopian sustainable community at Maryhill and took to constructing a mansion that he named for his wife. She apparently did not share his particular view of destiny and left him for the big city. Sam Hill is rich in posthumous loyalty however, as we roadtrippers remain ever grateful for his contributions to good roads. And for placing odd attractions and obscure European art objects right in the middle of nowhere—where we can find them!

Now wander off to the west about 25 miles from Maryhill to the community of Lyle, your entrance to the mouth of the Klickitat Canyon. As the fast-moving Klickitat River makes its whitewater drop into the gorge, local Native American fishermen still use salmon dip nets

like they did more than a century ago. As history would have it, white settlement and the building of forty-foot-high fish wheels down on the Columbia soundly disrupted this mindful and sustainable practice. These clever contraptions awaited the large fish as they migrated near shore, scooping them by the ton onto scows headed for the canneries downstream. Thus began the era of overfishing and resource depletion, and today science and society still struggle with our losses. Where nature and the environment are concerned, the past is ever present.

Driving north on State Highway 142, you'll twist and climb for about 20 miles through

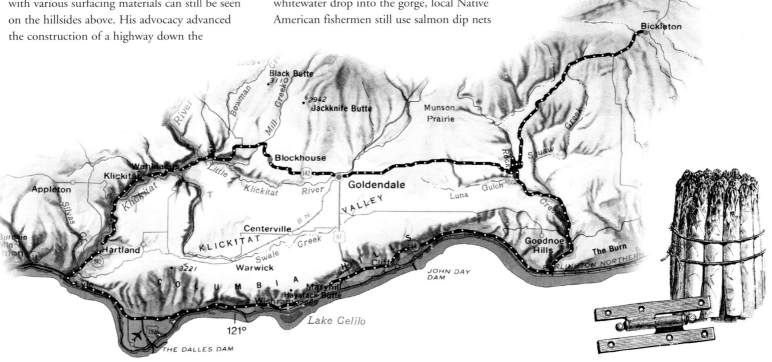

changing geography and altitude, topping out on the broad shoulders of Washington's south-central rim. On your way up, you'll pass a long-abandoned dry-ice factory alongside the river just north of the town of Klickitat.

The quaint towns of Appleton and Wahkiakus are worth exploring, or you can try your luck

Nearly snowless Mount Adams at summer's end

with a fly rod or steelhead pole in the Klickitat River's frigid waters, which rage down from the snowfields in the Goat Rocks. With breakfast in Glenwood you get a fine view of Mount Adams. More than once I have gazed out to the west from here and observed with a smile the thick gray edge of the marine cloud blanket that gathers up to the Cascade ridgeline and goes no further. Ah, to be on the sunny side!

Head east along the plateau, still on State Highway 142, into Goldendale. The Bickleton Road takes you out the other side of town, across Highway 97, and into some remarkable

scenery. The deep-emerald crowns of live oak trees contrast with the golden hillsides of the eastern Klickitat Valley. Halfway to Bickleton, the self-proclaimed "Bluebird Capital of Washington," the strikingly rugged Rock Creek Canyon commands some serious downshifting as you descend. Make a note that the unpaved road that splits south from the canyon bottom is your later return route to the Columbia.

Bickleton is charmingly typical of southeastern Washington farm towns. In the warm, late-summer quiet, one can imagine grange picnics and lots of overalls, but I saw no one this particular day. Not even a bluebird. Several magpies, however, were dancing on a fence by the old white-steepled church. The tranquility of this simple rural setting will move you. Lean against that old fence and drink in the moment. Maybe you could dangle a piece of straw from your mouth for that good old, down-home, peaceful, easy backroad feeling.

Reverse your direction and follow Rock Creek back to the wide Columbia. If you turn east on State Highway 14, the shoreline is more desolate. In fact, there's no gas station for sixty miles. Head west if you wish to return to relative civilization. And tip your hat to Sam Hill on the way past Stonehenge—he's buried on the bluff nearby. These backroads were his idea after all.

• Hometown •
KLICKITAT

One summer Saturday night some years ago, I drove from my camp up on the river to see what was happening in town. I grabbed a burger at the local grocery/drive-in/restaurant/hardware store and joined the crowds down the block at the city park. Sitting on spread-out blankets, folding lawn chairs brought from home, and rickety park benches, we all watched the forest fire burning high on the hillside across the river.

The night was very warm and still. Dark and quiet except for the distant flickering and crackling. Every so often a tree on the ridgetop would explode in flame and throw a glow on the audience. The kids lying on the grass would look up briefly with tired eyes. Their parents would pause a moment and then go back to their quiet small-town chat.

43

Pine-built remnants of the past near Chesaw

LOCATION:
- North-central Washington in Okanogan County
- Benchmark Atlas pages 46, 47
- One-way route from Tonasket through Loomis and Nighthawk then to Oroville, Molson, Chesaw, and ending at Old Toroda approximately 83 miles

SIGHTS AND SCENES
- The high hills and old mining country of the expansive Okanogan region
- Ghost towns and abandoned homesteads that tell enduring stories of a pioneer past
- Quiet valleys that fill the spaces between the highland hills with lushness and livestock
- Row upon row of apple trees making healthy sweetness out of the summer heat

FOLLOW ME:
- Beginning at Tonasket cross the river and drive Old Highway 7 South to the north about five miles
- Turn east on Loomis-Oroville Road to the town of Loomis
- Continue on along Palmer Lake and then down the Similkameen River past Nighthawk and to Oroville
- Cross through town and climb out of the valley to the east on the Oroville-Toroda Creek Road
- After 5-6 miles, take Nine Mile Road north to Sidley Lake and Molson
- Return to the Oroville-Toroda Creek Road on the Molson Road and turn east to Chesaw
- The same road continues east past Beaver Lake and ends at Toroda Creek Road
- Turn left about five miles to the ghost town of Old Toroda
- Return to the Okanogan Valley via Highway 20 or retrace your route to Chesaw and then south-west through Havillah and back to Tonasket

BACKROAD TRIP 10

IN SEARCH OF GOLD
High on the Okanogan Highlands

Colorful flowers brighten Brewster on the Okanogan River

A long-abandoned settlement rests at the foot of a slope below the county road. Ebony slats of hill-country pine side a barn and a scattering of smaller sheds in surprisingly fine order for their aged construction. A fellow traveler has stopped, and we stand there in consultation on the side of the road with arms folded.

The remark is made about how rustic roadside sights like this are much more frequent and undisturbed around here than anywhere else in the state. A couple of knowing nods, a photograph, a wave, and we go our separate ways.

I had come to the upper Okanogan a number of times before to explore this rare and remote region. The land is rugged, lusty, and just plain big, stretching from the Pasayten Wilderness to the Selkirk Mountains and south to the Columbia. It's not a spot you just drop in for a moment— it's a day's drive from Puget Sound. But I have learned, like the gold-seekers that swarmed the surrounding valleys and highlands years ago, that there is treasure to be found.

Hidden river valleys meld into high, grassy plains. Soon you're gazing at a cluster of long-abandoned pioneer farm buildings next to a reed-lined pond

that could as well be a mirage. Farther yet and you're in the ruins of a mining village that one hundred years ago was anxious and optimistic with the vices and dreams of half a thousand pilgrims.

The search for gold was fairly successful but temporary, and farming and ranching took over to support the newcomers. Today's orchards and commercial crops sustain a relatively sparse population. Long-time residents here are hardworking, content in their remoteness, and favor the outdoors. Here's what really invited my attention: Out in the hills you can still buy a spread for under a grand an acre, build your own homestead without hardly nobody watchin', and even stake a mining claim if that suits you. Now that's progress!

It was early morning in late summer as I departed the town of Tonasket for the hills. There had been talk of wildfires over in the Pasayten and

down on the Colville Reservation, but thus far the only heat was the August sun on my shoulders in the open-topped car.

I set out northwest for Loomis, which rests within orchard-fringed hills where the Sinlahekin River joins the Similkameen Valley below Palmer Lake. The town tells much of the story of all the small settlements that began in the Okanogan country in the late 1800s. The cattle companies arrived in these valleys and at first coexisted with the local tribes. As populations grew, pioneers began farming the land, disregarding the natives' long-standing presence. Gold miners who had trickled in from spent claims up north on the Fraser River found pockets of rich ore all about the north-central part of the state. From the 1880s to the mid-twentieth century, mines succeeded and failed; towns boomed and busted.

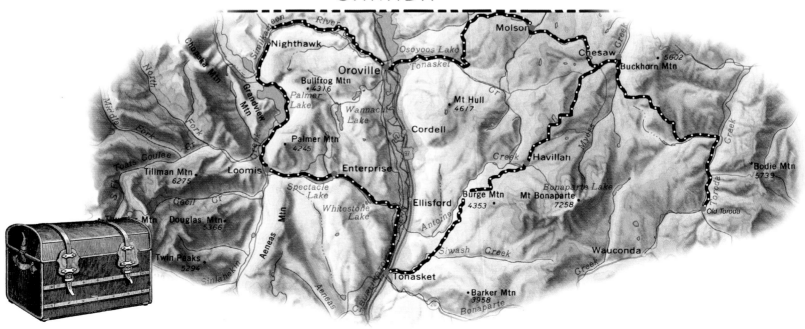

Away up the rocky draws and creases in the Similkameen are the ghosts of several once-productive lodes. Eventually, the Indians traded away rights to the land, the cattle ranches downsized, the mines closed, and apple orchards are now the less-contentious wealth of this peaceful and sensuous country.

Fall foliage in a lakeside park

Nighthawk is next on your journey through time. As you follow the Similkameen down, bending along with the irrigation chutes and the abandoned rail spur, look below the north-facing cliff as you cross the river. It's a movie set all too real—a couple dozen old frame structures in classic ghost town repose. All privately owned and unavailable for browsing, sad to say.

Once through Oroville I climbed the steep grade toward Chesaw and delighted in a bit of the coolness a couple thousand feet could provide. The well-maintained gravel of Nine Mile Road took me within a few feet of the international border. Along the way, I looked down on Oroville from a spot where the screaming Great

Northern steam engines used to stop and cool their brakes a century ago.

In Molson, the rusty machines of yesteryear scatter about the ancient townsite, welcoming all who pass to step back a century or so, and I surely couldn't resist. A hot wind sifted between the cracks in the old bank as I listened to ancient echoes. I checked my watch then looked at the strangely dappled sky. I shortly saddled up and moved on.

You must get to Old Toroda to view what was a bustling town of five hundred souls in 1898. Today it is but a monument of tilted pinewood cabins and sagging fences. You, too, can ponder how the construction remains so well preserved. I offer only speculation. The winters tend to be severe here and the summers are blistering, but maybe it's the nature of the wood and the quality of the assembly. Perhaps it's the absence of vandals and land development that have allowed this to be. Whatever the reason, these durable vestiges of past times are great gifts to the sense of place so prized by us backroaders.

It was 98 degrees as I took Hungry Hollow Road south out of Chesaw. In the west distance I could see the sky redden and haze. I eased the car past Havillah and the ski hill at Sitzmark, a most improbable sight on this blistering day. My car descended toward Tonasket as the lowering sun pierced a blood-red eye through the western sky.

Finally I could see the Okanogan below. The air grew heavy with smoke, and the heat became stifling. When I reached the river valley I was surrounded by a storm of ash and found the main highway closed due to one of the dozen lightning-spawned wildfires that were burning from Chelan to Nespelem and north to the border.

While praying for the best of outcomes for all involved, I marveled at one more show of nature's honesty and artistry to be found along the road.

• Hometown •
TONASKET

The motel sign urged me to stop and stay, promising that their beds were new and the coffee pot was always on. Always the daring King of the Road, I checked in. No phone, no pool, no pets. (No soap, no lock, no clock, no drinking cups…). I passed on the coffee, but they were right about the beds.

You have to love the honesty here. The local tavern is right next door to the food and clothing bank, and the police station is close by. In front of the station on the sidewalk under the awning are a few old wooden chairs. Seems to me you could just sit there a spell and maybe you and the chief can work this whole thing out.

One old fellow tells me in short, clipped sentences that the town hasn't changed much since he got here half a hundred years ago, and I believed him. The winters were still bitter cold and the mid-summer swelter knocks you down a notch or two. "It reminds me of hell—except the people are nicer."

An old corral waits out a storm near the Columbia River

LOCATION:

- *North-central Washington in Chelan, Douglas, and Okanogan Counties*
- *Benchmark Atlas pages 60, 62, 73, 75*
- *Route from Wenatchee to Okanogan backroads via Grand Coulee approximately 112 miles*

SIGHTS AND SCENES:

- *Sage-sided canyons up to the productive farms of the spacious Columbia plateau*
- *Miles of electrical transmission lines that lead you through the heat to Grand Coulee Dam*
- *Truly open roads under the biggest skies, and modest widely spaced towns*
- *Options for intrigue and adventure in the Colville backwoods*

FOLLOW ME:

- *From U.S. Highway 97 near the Beebe Bridge, drive up McNeil Canyon Road to the Waterville Plateau*
- *At the Mud Springs Road follow the signs to State Highway 172 and Mansfield*
- *Continue on 172 to Highway 17 then north 8 miles to Highway 174*
- *Proceed east on 174 to Grand Coulee Dam*
- *Depart Coulee Dam on State Highway 155 to journey into the Colville Indian Reservation and points north, or*
- *Retrace your route back to the Columbia across the plateau, or*
- *Sidetrip through Brewster by taking Hwy 174 to Bridgeport, then return to the river at Pateros*

BACKROAD TRIP

11

THE GREAT PLATEAU AND GRAND COULEE

Power in the Emptiness

Horses huddle against the eastern Washington wind

Touch the heart of Washington State and feel the magnificent plateau heat amid the wheat that blows free above the coulees. The mighty Columbia River encircles much of this roadtrip as it bends around the tableland we cross to reach Grand Coulee Dam. From there we'll head into the unpredictable vastness of the Okanogan and wonder what comes next.

The colorful orchards north of Wenatchee paint the basalt-walled slopes above the Columbia as you drive up U.S. Highway 97 from the south. Your first landmark is the Beebe Bridge which carries the highway back to the west side of the river. Here is where you break away! Instead of now following the crowds to Lake Chelan or Winthrop, hang a right just before the bridge and twist your car up the McNeil Canyon Road. Climb the scrub-lined grade for 5 amazingly steep miles and you'll top out in wheat country high on the Waterville Plateau. Follow the funky old road signs east to tiny Mansfield, which on approach appears as a mirage wiggling in the waves of August heat. Cruise slowly past false-fronted buildings on a dusty street lined with pickup trucks. The boys are waiting out the sweaty mid-afternoon over a cold one in the Mansfield Tavern.

Exiting town and continuing on Highway 172, then 17 North, then 174 East, you soon arrive at the doorstep of one of the largest concrete structures in the world. Grand Coulee Dam brought farming to the desert, cheap power to Kaiser and Boeing so we could win the big war, and a lake that extends all the way to Canada. The Visitors Center features fascinating exhibits about this engineering wonder and leaves you with a proper sense of prehistory, geology, progress, and industry. I have visited several dams, and though interesting and respectful, I always find their displays of native's lifestyles and their dependence on the free-flowing river a bit ironic.

The calm town of Coulee Dam rests pasted upon the north wall of the gorge. Tree-lined streets hum in the summer warmth. Wander down the hill and, for a break, take the Historical Walk along shady streets. You'll notice squeaky-clean blocks of smartly painted houses wrapped in wisteria vines. Three other towns circle the dam, all dating from construction days: Electric City, Grand Coulee, and Elmer City.

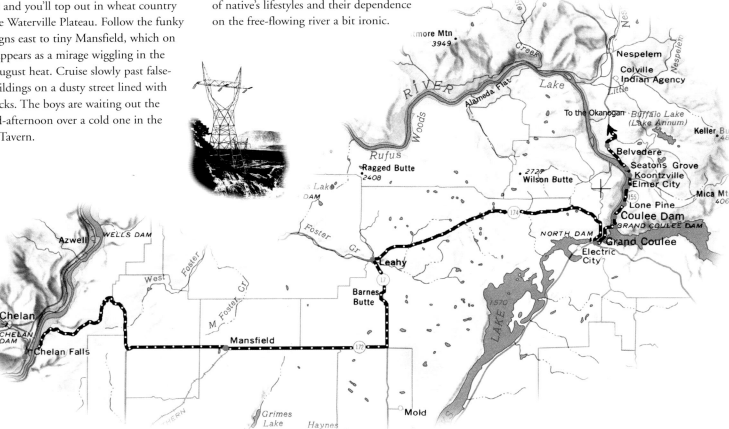

The surroundings here are otherworldly. The towns chiseled into the cliffs, the awesome bulk of cement wedged into the canyon, the tangled vortex of high-tension lines on steel towers. The whole scene is stunning with its man-conquers-nature grandeur, but it can leave one edgy. At night they fire a laser light show at the spillway. That's just a bit too otherworldly for me, and I moved on to less energetic surroundings.

Straight and silent backroad on the Columbia Plateau

If you're feeling adventurous, you can follow me north and east into the Okanogan forest with its hidden lakes and remote valleys. State Highway 155 takes you out of Coulee Dam and into the Colville Reservation and beyond to the Okanogan. From here on, the world is expansive and isolated, and you have your pick of roads seldom roamed by outsiders.

Dear traveler, you are not in Bellevue anymore! Backroads in these parts have a different flavor and cultural tilt. Folks may wave as you pass on roads that lead to hidden hollows, secret fishin' holes, and, true enough, the occasional anarchist homestead. Indeed, those that do not smile and wave may be living away from civilization for a reason, and you might do well to stick to the asphalt. It's probably a good idea to avoid examining any odd-looking crop you may stumble upon.

Then there was the time my car hitched a ride to Omak on the back of a tow truck having dared a washed-out culvert while trying to find the Sandpoil River. (Remember that when this book invites you to "follow me"!)

You can also simply retrace your steps across the plateau. Nothing like another sage-scented drive across those boundless fields. You can't surpass that magic feeling flying down those straight and seemingly endless roads. It's just you and the warm wind riding the up and down waves of asphalt and knowing when you get to the end of one road, another is there to take you somewhere else.

And now, if you really must, rejoin the crowds and the more traditional and mellow summer fun in Chelan or the Methow. Your love of open spaces and curiosity for the unknown has set you apart. Anyone can own a lakeside condo—you own the road!

● Hometown ●
MANSFIELD

You're on a movie set. The dusty streets and false-fronted buildings along main street suggest you wait for high noon just to see what might happen. No one needs to yell "Quiet on the set!" because no one is making any noise. Well, sure, a truck door slammed down by the feed store and the wind is blowing the metal sign around in front of the gas station, but that just adds to the scene.

The Great Northern Railway arrived here in the early 1900s. Unfortunately, Mansfield was located a couple of miles south at the time. The railroad assured prosperity and apparently it was a simple matter to move the town to where the rails ended. Sort of like that Hollywood back lot.

The dry yellow sun was directly overhead when they walked into the street. Both stopped to face each other in the dust and silence. As they approached each other, his hand went for his hip, lightning quick. The other man hadn't cleared leather before he was looking at the wallet photos of his buddy's new daughter. Another true hometown story of the Old West.

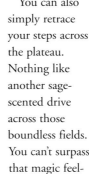

Ancient basalt walls cradle spring-fed Moses Coulee

LOCATION:
- Central Washington in Douglas County
- Benchmark Atlas pages 74, 60
- One way route from the entrance to Moses Coulee to Chief Joseph Dam approximately 61 miles

SIGHTS AND SCENES:
- A secluded and serene spring-fed valley that draws up to the high plateau
- The timeless spirit of a prominent native chief watching from the basalt bluffs above
- A hidden oasis with a waterfall that rushes beneath old trestle timbers up Douglas Creek
- A late afternoon sprint along plateau highways surrounded by glacier-sculpted scenery

FOLLOW ME:
- From State Highway 28, 13 miles south of East Wenatchee, take Palisades Road up Moses Coulee passing through the small villages of Appledale and Palisades
- The road turns to improved gravel and continues to the Billingsly Ranch where it becomes Road 24 NW
- Climb out of the canyon and then turn right on Sagebrush Flats Road 3 miles to Coulee Meadows (Rimrock) Road
- Proceed north to the end of Coulee Meadows Road at US Highway 2
- Go 6 miles west on US 2 and turn right on Washington 172 at Farmer
- Travel 12 miles north then 5 miles east to Mathieson Road
- Take Mathieson Road north 4 miles, then jog left one mile, then north to Bridgeport Hill Road
- Follow Foster Creek down to the river on Bridgeport Hill Road and Highway 17 ending at Chief Joseph Dam

TRAIL TO THE CHIEF
BACKROAD TRIP 12

Seeking the Past up Moses Coulee

Hidden falls and pool on Douglas Creek

Chief Moses is said to have been a most interesting man. He had no illusions that the natives of the northwest could challenge the invasion of white settlers that overwhelmed the Columbia Plateau 150 years ago. Moses made his peace, took his bribes of money and whiskey, as well as his five wives, and retreated home to the beautiful spring-fed valley that still holds his name. When you combine the stunning solitude of the surroundings with this provocative history, a slow drive up Moses Coulee becomes journey of the spirit.

You enter Moses Coulee at its gaping basalt mouth and immediately feel a magical serenity. The sage sweetens, the sky turns neon, the breeze chants in tones of blackbird, killdeer, and pheasant. Undistracted by traffic, you can see where last spring's waterfalls have scarred the chocolate cliffs. An old sun-baked homestead melts into the gold-brown hillside that tilts on its alluvial skirt of copper rock.

Deep-green fields of alfalfa give way to rows of apples. The aura of the valley deepens as you drive slowly inside. A peculiar soundlessness echoes; you feel invisible as if in a sci-fi Western movie. You don't belong, but you can't leave.

I spotted the old railroad grade that traverses the north coulee wall toward the mouth of Douglas Canyon. I couldn't resist. Climbing a beat-up road that dead-ends at the remains of an old trestle, I parked, then danced down the shale slope to take a quick dip in a hidden springwater pool at the base of a small falls.

I returned to the canyon floor across an untended field at the foot of a cliff where a half dozen old buses and trailers clustered communally and spoke of peaceful coexistence and splendid isolation. Chief Moses would be proud.

It's about twenty miles from the Columbia up the Palisades Road to the Billingsly Ranch where a dusty gravel switchback lifts you out of the coulee and east along Sagebrush Flats. Turn left on Rimrock Road and you'll re-cross the upper coulee at McCartney Creek and be on your way to the high plateau of dryland wheat, bundled hay, power transmission lines, and beautifully

lonely roads. Ice-age floods shaped this immense highland, and you can feel the petrified riffles with your car as you head north, passing nothing and no one.

You will intersect cross-state Highway 2 near milepost 171 where a sideroad continues up the high reaches of Moses Coulee to lonely Jameson Lake—worth a visit but a dead end. Turn west onto 2 and climb up the hill to the intersection with State Highway 172 at a place called Farmer where the last leg of the journey will return you to the Columbia River.

The Waterville Plateau is flat and fast. Set the compass for true north. The road reads straight as a narrow arrow. There is one wiggle about a mile beyond Withrow,

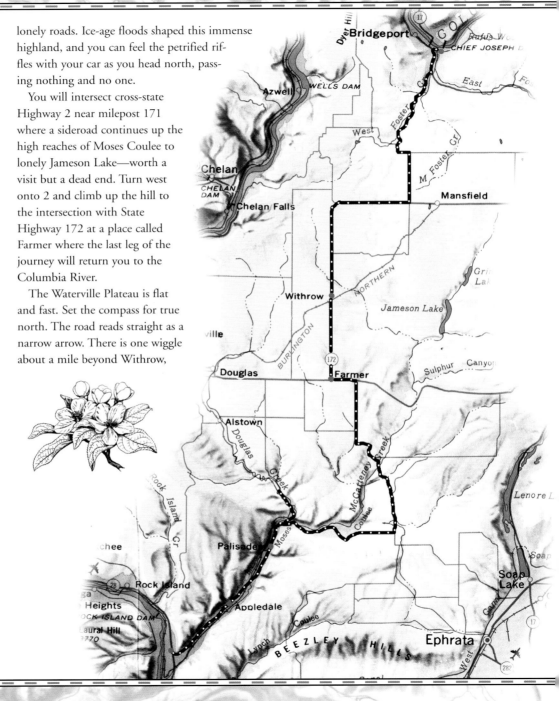

which allows for an immovable house-sized monolith dispossessed by some long-ago glacier.

State Highway 172 bends east, and after several miles I located Mathieson Road, which pointed me north to the plateau rim. I wandered a bit amid a series of hilly turns framed by the swirling furrows of wheat stubble then pulled over to consult the map. It was so quiet a person could hardly think. Just right.

Foster Creek lead me back to the Columbia at the foot of Chief Joseph Dam, which was named in honor of the peace-loving Chief Moses' more boisterous and war-like contemporary. I listened to the pounding din roaring from above and reflected on my pass through the tranquil valley earlier that day. It seemed fitting how appropriately the white man paid tribute to the disposition of each.

Orchards guard the entrance to Moses Coulee

55

• Hometown •
PALISADES

There's a dot and a name on the map, but often "downtown" is but a single building. If open, it is likely the only place to buy food. It might also hold the town post office, the best coffee around, or the state liquor agency. It may be someone's livelihood or simply a money-losing pastime that is too strong a habit to quit.

The Palisades Store sits on the road, stitched to its canyon wall backdrop. The scene invites you to wonder any number of things. Who runs the place? Who shops here? Where is everybody? I petted the horses in the corral across the road and considered walking up to the door and poking my head in. Maybe asking around a bit.

In the end I simply moved on. Everything I needed to know about the dot on the map named Palisades was revealed to me by studying that one old building with its full porch. Here is what I learned: Life is uncomplicated. Hard work always pays off. Folks here know how to talk out their problems. If you feel the need, it is alright to sit here on the porch and chat. The world is not meant to hurry or to change. And if you need anything, let us know. We just might be here.

Lower Crab Creek Valley and the springtime-green Saddle Mountains

LOCATION:
- Central Washington in Lincoln and Grant Counties
- Benchmark Atlas pages 75, 88, 89
- One-way route from Soap Lake through Moses Lake, Potholes, and along lower Crab Creek Valley to the Columbia River approximately 75 miles

SIGHTS AND SCENES:
- An enigmatic cross-state waterway that defies the heat and terrain as it weaves from near Spokane to the middle of nowhere
- Marshlands and seeps hosting migrating waterfowl and thirsty livestock
- A moonscape of desert dunes surrounding the Potholes
- The enchanting lower creek valley hidden from the real world by the shadow of the Saddle Mountains

FOLLOW ME:
- From the town of Soap Lake drive east 4 miles on County Road 20 NE to Crab Creek
- Proceed south on Road E NE, to Road 19 NE, then Road D7 NE, which becomes 16 NE after fording the creek
- Turn south on Stratford Road and drive through Moses Lake, merging onto State Highway 17 South
- Cross Interstate 90 and turn off Highway 17 onto Road M SE near McDonald, which takes you south 5.5 miles to O'Sullivan Dam Road, where you turn right
- Cross the dam and turn south on Road H SE over Frenchman Hills to Road 12 SE where you turn west to Road D SE and then south to State Highway 26
- Head east 1 mile and then take Road B SE to the Lower Crab Creek Road and turn right to explore the valley to its end at the Columbia River

GOING WITH THE FLOW
Chasing Down Crab Creek

BACKROAD TRIP 13

Perch Lake along the ancient route of the Columbia River

F ar out on the plateau, where the summer days dawn warm and bright and the horizons seem endless, you can do some most creative exploring. Crab Creek trickles through the sage like a misplaced water feature in a desert garden, and I long ago developed a curious urge to wander with this enigmatic waterway as it wiggles and twists across and down the Columbia Plateau. Crawl with me as we explore the strength and weakness, beauty and toughness, glory and desolation to be found in the warm heart of the state.

By the time I caught up with Crab Creek it had already meandered far from its source in the hills below Reardon not far from Spokane, pausing at ponds and grassy puddles and occasionally drifting July dry. At Odessa it meets the railroad and the disowned trails of yesteryear's cattle drives and continues on its westward journey.

I began after lunch in Soap Lake, coffee cup in hand, and boarded County Road 20 NE out to Gloyd Seeps. I broke off to the south on a gravel road astride the waterway. Soon I was wetting my hubcaps in the first of my Crab Creek crossings, the only one without the aid of a bridge. Presuming you too make it across, follow me south through Moses Lake, where long ago native peoples gathered to dig camas and biscuit-root and graze their horses on the once-abundant bunch grass. Today it's the great-great grandchildren of the white settlers who can be seen digging potatoes and baling alfalfa. Beyond Interstate 90 we will resume our pursuit.

Please bear with me as I offer this sketchy and vaguely scientific rendition of the hydrology of central Washington. The Columbia Basin Project saw its first dose of long-promised water in the year 1950. It was then that the wartime duty of full electricity production by Grand Coulee Dam was shifted to the huge pumps that raised the impounded water up to Banks Lake at the head of Grand Coulee. Gravity went to work pulling the water southward through man-made canals to transform the sage and grasslands into wheat, peas, grasses, and corn. As the water came to the land, newly created drainages, seeps, and lit-

tle lowland lakes called potholes sprouted between the Grand Coulee and the Saddle Mountains, recharging the path Crab Creek had taken through the glacier-carved channel for eons.

The Potholes region is wildly captivating. A million people a month pass by on the interstate not ten miles to the north, but next to no one ever comes calling. For those that do, off-road vehicles, shallow draft boats, or hiking boots take them to Arabian-like sand dunes and hidden warm sinks where I hear some fat and happy fish dwell. There's a small commercial area near the Potholes Dam where you can get

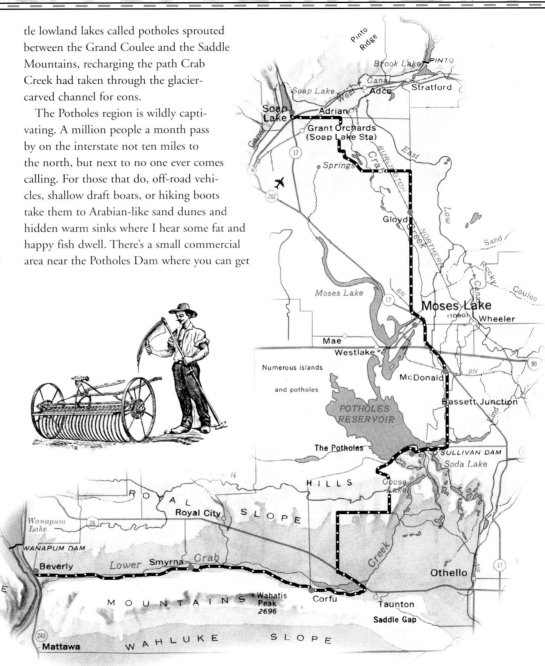

gas, a soda, and a pretty good haircut, as I discovered, before continuing south over Frenchman Hills.

Sun sets on a Mattawa vineyard

Having become one with Moses Lake and then the Potholes, Crab Creek now drizzles south among the Seep Lakes then exits as a respectable if slow-moving channel bending west. You might now guide yourself east on McMananon Road for a look at the ruggedly scenic Columbia National Wildlife Refuge, and this would take you through Othello. With all due respect, I'd seen enough in past travels of the potato factory farms and feedlots that one finds where the valley broadens to the southeast and beyond. If you long for a visit to the other side of the drive-thru window, be my guest. Me, I turned west onto the 12 SE Road then south on D Road SE and wandered awhile amid fields scented with mint and hay.

Backtracking east a few miles on State Highway 26 brought me to Gillis Road and the entrance to the Lower Crab Creek Valley—the best part of the trip. The slow gravel road winds astride the abandoned St. Paul and Milwaukee Railroad at the base of the steep shadow-banded slopes of Saddle Mountain. The journey overlooks verdant wetlands, home to migratory birds and occasional fields of grazing horses.

On two occasions I stepped out onto the shoulder and listened to the quiet. I ambled for a few hundred yards along the old electric railroad grade and watched finger-sized grasshoppers pop at my footsteps in the sage-scented valley warmth. Something was magical here; I invite you to visit and help describe what it might be.

The journey down Crab Creek Road from Highway 26 to the Columbia should take you about an hour. It will surely last longer if the coming sunset has blessed the valley with the color-bending glow of golds and reds as it did for me. A fitting conclusion to an honest summer's day spent down along the creek.

• Hometown •
SOAP LAKE

The cops here park a driverless patrol car where the highway hits the edge of town. I've heard it works well, people being what we are.

Some say the deception applies to the lake and its fabled healing waters. I tried them once and only got chilly and slickery. But maybe it's because I wasn't feeling ill at the time. I've seen more visitors working on their well-being at the Businessman's Club bar over the years. Annual dues are five bucks. They write your name in a big register, so it's no problem if you lose your card. Just for reference, Soap Lake is free.

I ate as always at Don's Restaurant. The waitress was stern and efficient: "There ya' go," she said as she lowered the roast beef and potatoes. Dessert came at the moment I chewed the last bite of beans. I was on the fast track.

After supper I strolled across the street and down the stairs to the club. I rang the bell, and the little wooden window slid open like in a speakeasy. It reminded me of going to confession many years ago. I told the bartender my name and she let me in. I guess if you're going to talk about your sins, they want you inside and seated.

Sturdy log pilings on the Pend Oreille River near Usk

60

LOCATION:

- *Eastern Washington in Stevens and Pend Oreille Counties*
- *Benchmark Atlas pages 63, 64, 65*
- *Route from Hunters across the Colville Valley to Usk on the Pend Oreille River and south to Chattaroy approximately 98 miles*

SIGHTS AND SCENES:

- *The warm sands of Lake Roosevelt where shoreline orchards meet the edge of the Selkirk Mountain foothills*
- *Deep forested ridges of Huckleberry Mountain where latter day homesteaders play out the drama of simpler times*
- *The calm, industrious Pend Oreille River among whose pilings paddlewheel steamboats once toiled*
- *Pine-trimmed gulches and glens in the hills north of Spokane where the used-to-be meets today*

FOLLOW ME:

- *Start at the community of Hunters and drive Washington Highway 25 north to Cedonia*
- *Head east on Cedonia-Addy Road over Huckleberry Mountain and down into the Colville Plain, Addy, and US Highway 395*
- *Drive south on US 395 10 miles to Chewelah*
- *Turn left on Flowery Trail Road over Chewelah Mountain*
- *When you reach the Pend Oreille valley and Calispell Lake follow the signs to Usk*
- *After you have seen Usk, proceed south on State Highway 211 to US Highway 2, turn east 3 miles to the Camden-Diamond Lake Road and turn right*
- *When you reach Camden, the road becomes Elk-Camden Road*
- *From Elk, take the Elk-Chattaroy Road south to Chattaroy and a return to Highway 2*

BACKROAD TRIP 14

BEYOND HUCKLEBERRY HILL

Spotlight on the Selkirks

Hunters Park on the Lake Roosevelt shore

The open road is your front-row seat to the drama of the world around you. The colored lines on the map and the alluring names of never-yet-seen villages can stir the imagination with hopeful expectation. And when the wheels start turning, you never really know how the story will go. This slow journey across the hills and valleys

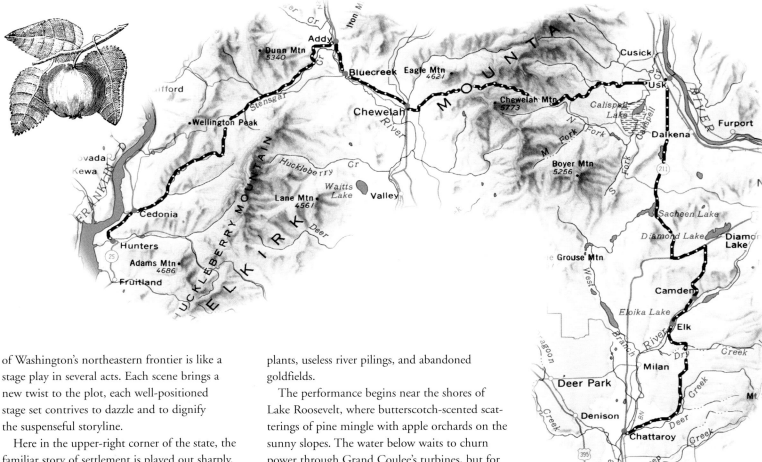

of Washington's northeastern frontier is like a stage play in several acts. Each scene brings a new twist to the plot, each well-positioned stage set contrives to dazzle and to dignify the suspenseful storyline.

Here in the upper-right corner of the state, the familiar story of settlement is played out sharply. This region held significant mineral deposits and abundant, easily harvested timber, and it is still seemingly wedded to its milling, mining, and refining history. It's as if this particular area did not develop much beyond the extraction boom years that slowed a century ago. Farming has proved unsteady, and relative remoteness has tended to freeze the scenes in time. The third replacement forest is greening the hills. Above graceful valleys, no-nonsense working communities hold fast near the remaining mills, cement

plants, useless river pilings, and abandoned goldfields.

The performance begins near the shores of Lake Roosevelt, where butterscotch-scented scatterings of pine mingle with apple orchards on the sunny slopes. The water below waits to churn power through Grand Coulee's turbines, but for now it hosts houseboats and swimmers enjoying the hot afternoon. The small upland town of Hunters remarkably resembles a Hollywood set. There is even a classic big-finned Plymouth convertible parked provocatively next to the old post office.

The Cedonia-Addy Road climbs a smooth valley to the shoulders of Huckleberry Mountain and you begin Act II—The Journey to the Unknown! Since my morning coffee down near Davenport, I had traveled from the wheat-

cloaked heartland, across the lakeshore headlands, now to these remote wooded highlands in the southern foothills of the Selkirk Range. The transition was most dramatic.

I crested the pass on Huckleberry Mountain and an astonishing stage prop caught my eye. A weathered plywood milk carton stands eight feet high on the shoulder of the road. My guess is that at one time this Darigold quart sheltered pint-sized school-bus riders from the rains that come prominently to this corner of the state.

I followed Stensgar Creek down into the town of Addy that sits just off US Highway 395, which is the hasty route from Spokane to Colville and the Canadian border. I poked around a few corners and saw the usual rustication, then drove down the Colville Valley to Chewelah, a fitting place for intermission and a tank of gasoline. I scanned the program in search of the next exciting scene. A cross street in the middle of town caught my eye. I took a left on Flowery Trail Road, the curtain rose, and I settled back in my seat.

Selkirk Mountains beyond the Colville Valley

It was up once more and over the high pass on Chewelah Mountain. I reached the turn off to the ski hill called 49 Degrees North—five hundred feet higher, by the way, than the state's most popular ski area. From there the performance really slowed down. Crews with monster trucks were rebuilding, repairing, realigning, and resurfacing a twelve-mile stretch of my chosen path.

Road construction is, of course, a familiar feature of backroad travel. The best thing is to alter your thinking rather than to become annoyed. Afterall, it's a safe road in good repair that you

want, right? And besides, backroad explorer, you aren't in a hurry anyway! So relax, observe, admire, and be thankful. As the pilot car guides you slowly along the route, take the time to watch how it's done. It's exciting, just like a free backstage pass! (You're not convinced. I can tell….)

The Pend Oreille Valley spreads ahead as you coast down and across the flats to the town of Usk (named for a river in Wales, they say). The Pend Oreille River is a waterway that was born to work. Flat and wide and flowing slowly, it was well suited for the stern-wheeled steamboats that marched continuously between the mills and markets in past years. Logging made a chain of boomtowns of Dalkena, Cusick and on up to Tiger and Ione. Wood products still have hold of Usk, with a good-sized lumber mill along State Highway 20 and a huge newsprint company just out of town.

State Highway 211 takes you due south. Soon you meet U.S. Highway 2 and are in a vacuum of autos that would suck you into Spokane if you aren't careful. I dodged the crowds and exited stage east to Diamond Lake, where I found the backroad route to Camden, Elk, and Chattaroy.

Elk rests in an amiable pine-trimmed valley astride the Little Spokane River. Until the 1930s things really got busy around here. The railroad and a huge sawmill had things hopping until the Depression. All the industry headed into Spokane, and again I made up my mind not to follow. As I reached Chattaroy and saw a preview of the fine and fancy homes of big city commuters, I chose to bring the curtain down. I turned around and headed back into the countryside.

Three rivers, two mountain ridges, a full program of exotically named towns, and a dozen well-rehearsed two-lanes in one afternoon. That's good theater!

• Hometown •
CHEWELAH

They're selling new shoes right there on the highway for twenty bucks a pair. Rows of box-covered card tables take up a whole city block— the better part of downtown. It's all here in Chewelah. You can get a banana latte at the Flowery Trail Coffee House, head down the road for a new Carhartt jacket at the Fantasy Farm and Feed, and pick up last season's newest Nikes out on the shoulder of the road.

On the backstreets near the Yu-Du-We-Du Laundromat, kids on bikes rule. They zip and holler up one shady block and down another. Past the gold-steepled church and back—daring summer to just try to come to an end before they've spent all their youthful energy.

Further up the hill on the edge of town, the cemetery rests. There's a plot for each sect and a fence between every persuasion. You'd think at some point we'd learn to get along.

Roadside chapel in Mt. Hope

64

LOCATION:

- Eastern Washington in Spokane and Whitman Counties
- Benchmark Atlas pages 78, 79, 92, 93
- One-way route from Dishman and Opportunity to Rockford, then across the hills to Plaza and ending at Rosalia, approximately 41 miles

SIGHTS AND SCENES:

- Mile upon mile upon mile of world-class golden wheat
- Asphalt, gravel, and seasonally adjustable dust-mud roads that entice you to get entirely lost
- Scenes of farming culture that spans a million acres and a half dozen generations
- The forever one of a kind villages of Rockford, Mt. Hope, Spangle, Plaza, and Rosalia

FOLLOW ME:

- Take the Dishman-Mica Road out of Spokane Valley and merge with State Highway 27 about five miles south of Opportunity
- Near Rockford turn right onto Valley Chapel Road
- Past the village of Mt. Hope turn south onto Kentucky Trails Road
- Cross Hangman Creek and explore the small valley on any collection of sideroads and summer roads
- Where Kentucky Trail ends at the Spangle Road, cross over to North Pine Creek Road, then Davis Road, which will take you to the Old Palouse Highway
- Drive south slowly between the rail tracks and the new highway to your destination in Rosalia
- You can return to Spokane on Highway 195 or move on west to the scablands or south toward Colfax and Palouse where you can catch Highway 27 back to the Spokane Valley

BACKROAD TRIP 15

RUNNING LOOSE IN THE PALOUSE

Summer Roads to Simplicity

An endless carpet of golden soft white wheat

I sit on the roadside near the old rail junction at Freeman. Before me was Backroad Nirvana, where tight, shoulderless two-lanes honeycomb the rolling countryside. Like the world's largest paved corn maze—except all I see is wheat. So many backroads, so little time!

The famous Palouse Hills shouldn't be missed. It is high on every travel writer's must-visit list. I usually tend to bypass the obvious and try to take you off the main path, but this spread of golden real estate has long been a favorite. The region that stretches south of Spokane to the Snake River is famous for its dryland crops, the gifts of ideal soil and a balanced climate. Join me as we set out to experience the deeper abundance along the sideroads and within the small communities of this special place.

I had come down from the Spokane valley town of Opportunity, having had to backtrack over to Highway 27 upon meeting the unforeseen temporary closure of the Dishman-Mica Road. An alternative route is to find the Palouse Highway down the backside of Spokane's south hill. Whichever route you favor, you are into the calm of the countryside before you know it.

From Freeman, little more than a sign in the road, I drove as if I knew where I was going. A couple years back I journeyed from Clarkston up Highway 27, skirting the Idaho border, following the rail line and streambeds and peeking at the quaint towns along the way. Today I'll head for the heart of the golden hills.

Out of Rockford I chose a turn onto Valley Chapel Road, the kind of name that would tempt any serous backroader. Soon I was stopped on a wheat-topped ridge with camera pointed at a postcard of rolling beauty, Mica Peak in the distance. The same undulating scene stretched out to each horizon. One wonders how these millions of acres all get harvested.

I don't know for sure because I didn't ask, but the prim white clapboard church in the settlement of Mt. Hope may indeed have been the "valley chapel" for which the road was named. It no longer mattered, as now you and I are heading south on Kentucky Trails Road, and we're headed for Hangman Creek.

I got good and turned around where the creek ravine cuts among the hills. In a shady grove of cottonwoods near one of my aimless crossings stands the monument to the event for which the stream is named: the tragic legacy of soldiers firming up the question of what role the Indians would play in their view of progress.

Should you get away from the blacktop as you meander, you may find yourself on one of many dusty trails that shortcuts through the chaff. Dusty, that is, until it rains. Then you're sunk. The mud in these parts is world class, just like the soil itself—hence the label "Summer Roads." Many are marked as such, while others are simply local knowledge. If you get stuck and need help, people are amazingly sparse. Should you reach a tow truck company on your cell phone and explain that they should come right on out to Summer Road, expect ringing laughter to echo across the golden rolling hills.

I rocketed down one of these farm trails, eagerly pushed forward by a massive ball of dust, just like slicing into meringue, and somehow found Kentucky Trails again and reached the Old Palouse Highway after a couple more shortcuts. Heading south I could see the "new and improved" US 195

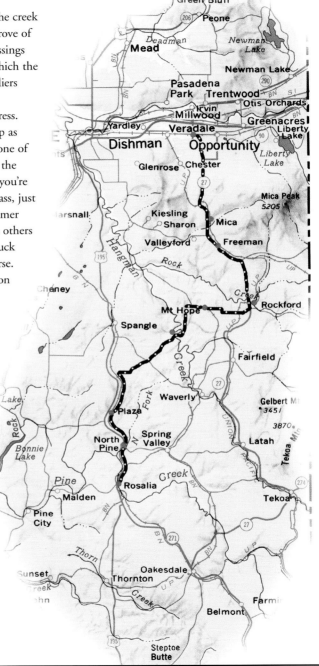

on the hillside to my right. This is great! I'm in a parallel universe. A roadtrip dream come true—a Designated Backroad!

I pass Pop wearing his best overalls and faded work shirt as he drives the wheat combine north along the highway—half on the shoulder, half on the road. Right behind him, blue-silver hair piled up high, is Mom at the wheel of the family one ton. Not much farther was a full parade of mammoth harvesters coming at me. One proud kid in an oversized straw hat waved. He was all of ten years of age, I swear. You in a hurry to get somewhere? Take that fast and fancy road up there. This here highway's only for roadtrippers, hardworking children, anyone wearing overalls, and truck-driving grandmas.

I soon arrived in Plaza, seemingly abandoned like so many of the small towns with their grain elevator and rail siding. The wheat harvest was winding down, but there was still obviously much to do. Long days, neighbors pitching in with one another, and sturdy non-stop equipment—it somehow all gets done before the fall rains come calling. I was here only to temporarily immerse myself in the rare scenic wonder of these Palouse Hills. The hardworking farmers that have raised wheat, peas, lentils, and seed here for generations understand well that the beauty that touched me is far more than skin deep.

The last stop is Rosalia. It is midafternoon and the heat that rises off the land spins a breeze down the slow streets. I could see a few folks idling on their porch steps beneath the shade of a large tree. There were kids wandering around town. One young guy in goggles is racing along on his bike with a snorkel protruding from his mouth, and I presumed the city pool down by the old school must be open. As he went to cool off, I spun the compass dial and headed deeper into the wheat.

An old spur line wanders the hills outside of Rockford

● Hometown ●
VERADALE

My grandfather was raised out here in the valley. At the age of eleven his parents, who could not support all their children, gave him to a better-off family to work on their farm. He took their name, and, for his own survival perhaps, became theirs. That's the way it was done back then, I guess.

As I drive Sprague Avenue out into the valley, the sweet memory of summer visits to my grandfather's small truck farm in Veradale stir to life. He never left the valley, and he hardly talked at all, but he would go fishing in the surrounding lakes whenever he could.

One at a time I pass through the shambled hearts of the previously distinct communities that once formed a well-spaced chain from Spokane to almost Idaho. Old downtowns and identities now smothered by progress: Dishman, Opportunity, Veradale, Greenacres, Liberty Lake. Now no longer very proud or defined. Taken in by the modern sprawl of the tax-base flowing upriver. The City of Spokane Valley, so the sign reads. The Inland Empire strikes back. A sacrifice of the nearly unthinkable, like passing off a family member to make life easier. Ah, but that's the way it's done now, I guess.

Washtucna rests calmly at the doorstep of the Scablands

LOCATION:
- *The southeastern Washington in Adams and Whitman Counties*
- *Benchmark Atlas pages 91,92*
- *One-way route from Washtucna to Rock Lake approximately 68 miles*

SIGHTS AND SCENES:
- *Rocky coulees, basalt cliffs, and dust devils dancing in the fields of hard-scrabble farms*
- *Benge, Winona, Lamont, and Ewan— uncomplicated hamlets set in stone within the irregular scenery*
- *The Palouse River, which somehow seems to be flowing uphill within this multi-level landscape*
- *Rock Lake, a most suitably named hideout from the heat after an afternoon of coulee crawling*

FOLLOW ME:
- *Begin at Washtucna and find State Highway 261 east of town and head north*
- *Veer right onto Benge-Washtucna Road to Benge*
- *Continue on Benge-Winona Road, which changes names to Endicott West Road and delivers you to Winona*
- *Backtrack across the Palouse River a quarter mile and take the Lancaster Road northeast to the town of St. John*
- *Turn west on Highway 23 to Ewan and turn right on Rock Lake Road and proceed about a mile and a half to the lake shore*

SCABLANDS MELODY
Smoothing Out the Rough Edges

Road and rail weave down toward Saint John

There's a stone-faced and ancient bank at the tiny junction of Winona in western Whitman County that you've got to see. Long closed and trying hard not to be noticed, it stands as a symbol and victim of its rough and rocky surroundings.

I set out on a white-hot afternoon to explore this basaltic

moonscape of canyons, coulees, and buttes bordered by the Snake River to the south, the rich and famous Palouse to the east, and the less rugged flats and farm fields to the west and north.

Washtucna is dug into a rocky notch where railroads crisscross the lonely roads that wiggle in from places like Dusty, Starbuck, and Kahlotus. My route took me north up Staley Coulee and into the heart of glacier-scoured back alleys in search of obscure beauty in this land scarred and disregarded.

A past sidetrip taught me some about the three-times tried and abandoned attempts to irrigate this region in the 1800s. All manner of dams, diversions, and ditches failed to overcome the general unwillingness of this obstinate territory. The remnants of these engineering flops can be seen between Washtucna and Hooper to the east.

The hoped-for farm-country rurality can be found alongside the road to Benge: a heavily weathered farmhouse dripping torn tarpaper next to a broken-bladed wind pump topped with a large nest. The scene looked like page 46 out of *The Grapes of Wrath*.

Where the rich loess soil manages to reach sufficient depth, fields are combed and styled into great mounds of swizzled cocoa-colored soil alternating with glowing grain.

The ride through these aptly named Channeled Scablands of southeastern Washington is uneven and pleasantly unnerving. To deal with the irregular geology,

whether a road builder or a farmer, you have to take what is given. The two-lane is hypnotically wrinkled, and the fields and pastures tilted and misshapen. As I twisted along, cautious and entranced, I found an old Grateful Dead tape deep in the console under some maps—a most suitable soundtrack to my meander. The edgy, dissonant harmonies and rocky lack of syncopation reflected the peculiar beauty of this rough and lyrical landscape, and I sang along with the hum of the tires.

When I drove into Winona, it all appeared as incurably empty and fatigued as that abandoned bank. But this spot

was surely bustling in the days of the Old Mullan Trail, which in the late 1800s was the principal route between the large fort at Walla Walla and western Montana. The railroads eventually supplanted the old wagon road, but they too are now mostly abandoned.

The one steel

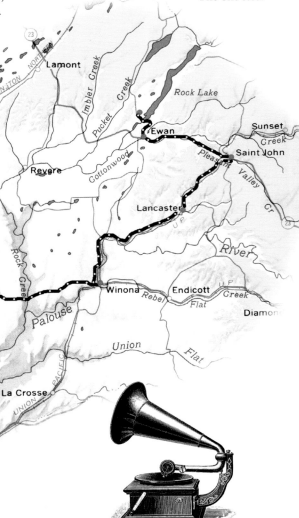

track that remains may well be the single element in this land with some predictability and clear purpose.

Each community along the road, with its grain elevator, rail siding, tavern, and school, is a knot in a two-lane asphalt weave that meshes together the eastern middle of Washington. A century and

Railside grain elevator at Winona

a half ago, agriculture, commerce, and socialization demanded this intriguing equidistance. This is the small town fabric that, even to this day, gives rural America its strength.

I joined the slow-flowing Palouse River and headed upstream on the Lancaster Road. Over that ridge to the east lie the smooth-rolling hills

of the Palouse and its deep soils that promise can't-fail wealth. Ever the posterchild for the glossy tourist magazines, the Palouse Region is where the wheat flows like gold spun well; not bludgeoned by granite schists.

The scablands are the "anti-palouse." It is no easy task to raise your crops and cattle where the land fights back with passive-aggressive shrugs. Scabland folks stand up to the abuse. These are the descendants of the "down-winders" after all. Whatever punishments the breezes from the Hanford Nuclear Reservation bestowed upon this region, you can't get tougher than trying to farm rocks. And the people I saw along the road owned the look of the land. Tanned, weathered, and solid like the basalt—unchanged and unchanging, clear in purpose and character.

From Lancaster, a tight and clean little town along the Union Pacific tracks, I veered north toward St. John where Washington Highway 23 crosses your path to take you west to Sprague and Interstate 90 or east to Dusty and the Palouse Highway. Following the rockier path, I wandered five miles to the northeast and into Ewan, little more than a white steepled church wedged along Rock Creek. From here it is two miles up to Rock Lake. Shore fishermen teased the perch and drank their beer in the baking heat. I had a quiet moment beneath the bronze cliff walls, took a picture and a quick swim, then headed to Ritzville for the night.

• Hometown •
ENDICOTT

Wooden slats, old brick, and tobacco-tinted stucco bounce the glow of day's end around empty corners. I follow the dusk into the heart of the town, stopping to catch the last glint of day coming from high on the trackside grain elevator as twilight takes over.

This is Endicott on a summer Sunday evening. But it might be Harrington, George, Lind, La Crosse, or Ritzville. All different but all so much the same: Wilbur, Prescott, Warden, Sprague, Othello, Connell, and the others. Drawing strength and permanence from their similarities: farms and wheat, rolling hills, and heat.

All these towns were born and boomed and grew prosperous a hundred years back. Now they've eased into the comfortable wisdom of elderhood. A history and destiny of simple ways and durability. Lazy but always on task.

The café closes early on Sunday evening, and I walk the downtown streets alone. Doors are open, and not a soul in sight. An old gauze drapery flutters out a second story window. Just like the Twilight Zone. And the same show is playing in Davenport and Schragg and Waterville and Reardon and Kahlotus and Washtucna and all the rest. Tomorrow all will again set about to work the land and mark life with each passing freight train and golden sundown.

The rolling grasslands of southeast Washington

LOCATION:
- *Southeast Washington in Columbia and Garfield Counties*
- *Benchmark Atlas pages 105, 106*
- *Loop route from Waitsburg about 83 miles*

SIGHTS AND SCENES:
- *The beautifully diverse landscape that rolls between the Snake River and the Blue Mountains*
- *Wheat fields, grain elevators, lazy rivers, steep gulches, and hidden hollows*
- *Dayton, Pomeroy, and Waitsburg, still dressed for 1910, the way all small farm towns should look*
- *Some mild mountain climbing with high views of green and gold-hued horizons*

FOLLOW ME:
- *Drive Cannery Road north out of Waitsburg 1 mile to Whoopemup Hollow Road. Go left and follow to end*
- *Turn right onto Whetstone Road which will take you northeast to Highway 12*
- *Cross over the highway and you will be on State Route 126 which takes you to Marengo*
- *From Marengo continue on SR 126 up the hill to Highway 12 and turn right to Pomeroy, about 5 miles*
- *Follow Dutch Flat Road south out of Pomeroy to Skyhawk Hill Road, turn right onto Tatman Mountain Road, then left on Niebel Gulch Road*
- *Turn left when you get to Bartels Road, wind around till you find Blind Grade Road, which takes you out of the hills and down to the Tucannon River*
- *Proceed south on the Tucannon Road for about 10 miles and turn to the right onto Forest Road 4620*
- *Continue up into the hills, and you will soon find yourself on Skyline Drive*
- *At the summit junction, you'll find Ecklar Mountain Road, which takes you down to Mustard Hollow and into Dayton where Highway 12 returns you to Waitsburg*

ON THE EDGE OF THE BLUES

Tales from the Exotic Far East

The Tucannon River east of Starbuck

"PRIMITIVE ROAD. NO WARNING SIGNS" read the warning sign—I knew I had found the right road!

I had just come up Whoopem-up Hollow on my way out into the corrugated hills of wheat that stretch north and east from Waitsburg. Some bumpy miles back, while

I was busy splashing coffee all over myself, a jacked-up pickup with two whoopin' teenage boys came speeding at me, bouncing mightily in a ball of dust that blocked out the morning sun. We missed colliding, but it was close. I figured if I could survive Whoopem-up this day, no road was too daunting.

The far southeast corner of Washington is a region of the simplest grandeur. Here you'll find small, friendly towns loosely linked by miles of roads that snake through honey-colored hills as you prowl hidden canyons and endless acres of quiet and suprising vistas.

Today you will touch both the heat of the hollows and the cool pine ridges of the Blue Mountains, which anchor the lower right corner of Washington onto Oregon and Idaho. This collection of backroads rides like a two-lane roller coaster. The ticket booth is in Waitsburg, but you can also climb on from the cities of Pullman and Clarkston to the east, or by dropping down from Interstate 90 around Ritzville.

At the end of Whoopem-up Hollow, turn onto the Whetstone Road and ride the hills east to intersect Washington Highway 12. Sneak over to the other side onto Turner Road. Oh boy, a shortcut! Drive bravely past the sign that reads Not Advisable for Through Traffic and wander northeast on this well-maintained gravel road. Wave to those you pass. It's the law.

The small former community of Marengo sits on the green banks of the incredibly curvy Tucannon River and may be the most idyllic spot in the state for pure isolated beauty. Scattered about this old crossroad I found broken barns and neglected sheds imploded by heat and time. The weary brown weathered boards were sharply grained and seemed eager to tell old stories.

A wiry gentleman beckoned me to the roadside while smiling around his corncob pipe. We shared maps and vagabond stories. He wished to know the condition of the road from the direction I had come. On his visit to Hell's Canyon the day before, his rental car suffered two blowouts, and though he preferred backroads, he didn't wish to spend another day awaiting assistance and listening to his wife's suggestions about where and how to drive.

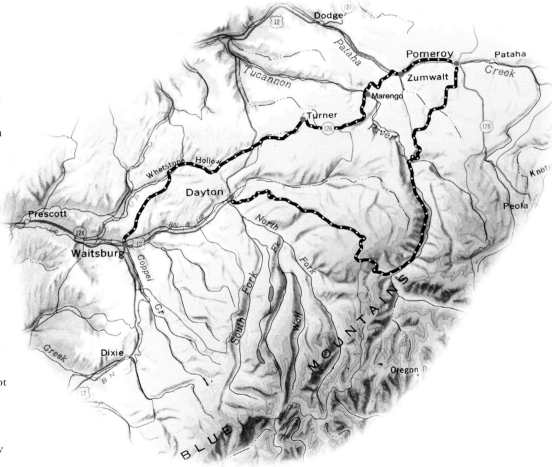

Despite my assurances, he chose the paved path. I watched him head south along the Tucannon and, no doubt at his wife's urging, soon back to Missouri. I pressed on up the steep and narrow grade to Pomeroy.

Pomeroy, Washington, is as whistle clean as a town can get. It sits calmly along Pataha Creek minding its business and raising its families. Like so very many small towns lacking visible indus-

Rusty wheel and weathered barn

try, it seemingly survives on its integrity and rural intelligence. Stop for a shady lunch in the local park, then fill your tank and water bottle and check your maps. You are now headed for the hills.

Dutch Flat Road heads due south from town into a lot of nowhere. Follow the map as you jog and weave your way back to the Tucannon River on Blind Grade Road. The Tucannon Road is paved and well-traveled, but don't worry, you won't have to be on it long! The next leg takes you into the Blues.

Two miles south of Camp Wooten State Park, turn right onto Forest Road 4620 and get ready to rattle and dust. If you're game, you'll get way the heck up the piney shoulders of this remote range. Reasonably maintained logging roads will get you over the top and back to Dayton on the Ecklar Mountain Road. But if you don't have fairly sturdy wheels, or if your teenager can't manage to be out of cell phone range for that long, just skip the forest and take the Tucannon Road out of the hills and back to State Highway 12.

Dayton is a great place to get gas, a car wash, and a cold one. As history has it, this is the location of the state's first high school and its last original railroad depot. When you've seen enough, follow the Touchet River downstream back to where you began in Waitsburg.

Toward the end of my day I headed on south toward Walla Walla and reached the small community of Dixie in late afternoon. Around me for miles the golden stubble of harvest alternated with brown fallow hills like gilded vanilla swirled through chocolate soil. I scanned the east horizon and the Blue Mountains, indeed blue, framed a colorful portrait of this fine backroad day.

• Hometown •
WAITSBURG

You can't get close to the southern border of Washington without numerous reminders that a traveling act named Lewis and Clark had once chanced to pass through. The Corps of Discovery apparently was granted branding rights to most of the geography here—from the town of Lewiston next to Clarkston, to the Lewis River in Clark County and on to the Lewis and Clark Wildlife Refuge. Fine tribute, but a bit redundant.

The expedition passed through this area in spring of 1806. Tired of fighting river rapids, the expedition came inland and took a shortcut up the Touchet River. After a tough winter short on food, they found fresh game and edible roots in the surrounding hills. They also hobnobbed with the locals, refusing the fine salmon that was offered, but curiously partaking of the dog.

Many years ago a friend and I formed our own Corps of Discovery reenactment. We floated down the Touchet in innertubes from Lewis and Clark Trail State Park (see what I mean?) to Waitsburg on a triple-digit July day. Ducking the barbwire strung across the low-running stream, losing half of our provisions, and portaging around cattle. Not only did we have to hitchhike back barefoot, but to this day no one has named anything after us!

Washington Pass and North Cascades Highway

REFERENCES AND SUGGESTED READING

The following publications and resources provided inspiration and information
for this book and are recommended for your further knowledge and enjoyment.

Blue Highways: A Journey Into America
By William Least-Heat Moon (William Trogdon). Little, Brown,
and Co., 1982.
The quintessential inspiration for those who seek soulfulness and truth
on the open road. A masterpiece by the true king of the gypsies.

Country Roads of Washington
By Archie Satterfield. Sammamish Press, 1989.
Previously released in 1980 as *Backroads of Washington* by this legendary
northwest author who was both guide and inspiration in my early years
of Evergreen State exploration.

Exploring Washington's Past: A Road Guide to History
By Ruth Kirk and Carmela Alexander. University of Washington Press, 1990.
The bible of backroad Washington. Complete, accurate, stimulating,
and expertly written.

The Good Rain: Across Time and Terrain in the Pacific Northwest
By Timothy Egan. Vintage Books, 1991.
The Northwest seen through the eye of a true adventurer, environmentalist,
and thoughtful social critic. Some of my reflections on man's indiscretions
against nature flowed from worthy writings like this.

Manifold Destiny: The One, The Only, Guide to Cooking on Your Car Engine!
By Chris Maynard and Bill Scheller. Villard Books, 1989, 1998.
Did I forget to mention how great dinner cooked under the hood
can taste after a long roadtrip?

Riverwalking: Reflections on Moving Water
By Kathleen Dean Moore. Lyons and Burford, 1995.
When you want to feel the earth and know sense of place, this is the
stuff you read. Especially if you love rivers as much as some of us do.

Traveler's History of Washington: A Roadside Historical Guide
By Bill Gulick. Caxton Printers, 1996.
In-depth coverage of lesser-known historical sites and events with an
interesting focus on industry and technology, pioneer to present.

Washington for the Curious: A By-the-Highway Guide to the Evergreen State
By Rob McDonald and Shawn Carkonen. The Curious Corporation, 1996.
The easy to reference format guides your way along each of the state's
roads describing towns and points of interest mile by mile.

Washington Road & Recreation Atlas
Benchmark Maps, 2002.
This invaluable guide was the primary source for the routes and descriptions
accompanying the roadtrips. Their cartographers also produce the Raven
Maps from which the chapter maps were derived.

The Wet Side of the Mountains
By Bill Speidel. Nettle Creek Publishing, 1974.
A classic, and the first of its kind. Not at all out of date if you want a
fascinating replay of what we in Western Washington were thinking a
quarter century ago.

John Deviny, a life-long resident of Washington state, has a keen and experienced eye for the wisdom of nature and the allure of the less ordinary. A self-proclaimed "itinerant social theorist," Deviny seeks to uncover the stories in the scenery while endorsing a more thoughtful and simplistic attitude toward the journey of life. He has written articles and stories on local lore for regional publications in his hometown of Olympia. This is his first book.

BOOK ORDERING INFORMATION

Here is how you can order additional copies of *Exploring Washington's Backroads*:

- Copies can be ordered through our website at:
  www.WashingtonBackroads.com

- Send your order to:

  Book Order/Wilder Productions
  P.O. Box 1848
  Olympia, Washington 98507-1848

  Please include your phone number
  and email address

- Check the "Northwest Travel" section of
  your local bookstore or online bookseller

- Bulk order and educational
  discounts available

Exploring Washington's Backroads

Prairie fenceline near Goldendale